SECOND EDITION

MAKING THE GRADE

HOW BOARDS CAN ENSURE ACADEMIC QUALITY

By Peter T. Ewell

Library of Congress Cataloging-in-Publication Data

Ewell, Peter.

Making the grade : how boards can ensure academic quality / by Peter T. Ewell. — 2nd ed. rev.
and updated.

p. cm.

Includes bibliographical references and index.

ISBN 978-0-926508-23-1 (alk. paper)

1. Universities and colleges--United States--Evaluation. 2. Universities and colleges—United
States—Administration. 3. Quality assurance--United States. I. Title.

LB2331.63.E94 2012

378.1'01--dc23

2012019346

*For more information on AGB Press publications or to order
additional copies of this book, call (800) 356-6317 or visit the AGB Web
site at **www.agb.org/publications**.*

CONTENTS

FOREWORD

Traditionally, boards have treated the product of their institutions—education—as off-limits. Whether out of deference for the role of faculty or from a belief that they are ill-equipped to explore questions of educational quality, board members typically have operated on the assumption that their domain is oversight of all other areas of the institution or system—that is, the financial, physical, policy, and leadership environments for education—but not the education itself. As a result, board members have tended to know little more about the education provided by their institutions than what they hear from successful students and proud faculty and administrators.

Given the current climate for higher education, boards need to develop new habits related to academic quality. The competition among colleges and universities for students, faculty, leaders, and grant and philanthropic dollars requires that boards be part of the conversation about the quality of their institutions' education and graduates. Institutions cannot position themselves competitively without the ability to make (and support) claims of excellence, claims that require supporting details and data. Boards seeking to move their institutions to a higher level or striving to define a clearer niche in the educational marketplace can do so effectively only if they can have strategic discussions about academic quality, raising appropriate questions and responding to appropriate information.

There are other, larger reasons for boards to become more informed and involved in matters related to education. For higher education, the 21st century began with a demand for greater board accountability. The public, including policy makers, raised the bar for boards of colleges and universities: Not only did it expect boards to deliver on their fiduciary responsibilities, it also demanded that boards be responsive to institutions' various constituents as well as be responsible for and to institutions and the public trust. Since that time, the public's demands have become more specific and more pressing. Parents, students, donors, and policy makers are now asking pointed questions about the value of higher education: Why does a college education cost so much? What's the return on the investment? How well prepared is a graduate for the world of work? Such questions demand that boards provide answers.

As a result of these pressures, board members can no longer demur when questions arise about the quality of the educational experience at their institution or in their system. According to AGB's 2010 survey on how boards oversee educational quality, there is both good news and bad on this front. First, the good news: Since the early 2000s, more than 50 percent of boards increased the amount of time they devoted to discussions of student learning. But the bad news is that nearly two-thirds of boards say they still do not spend enough time on the topic. Given the pressure to respond to public questions about quality and the need to compete in the marketplace, more board engagement is crucial. But many boards, as well as presidents and chief academic officers, struggle with questions of how to achieve this engagement: How can board members become appropriately informed about educational quality given their diverse professional backgrounds? How can boards use their time efficiently and effectively in reviewing information about educational quality? How can boards best use their authority to ensure quality without micromanaging the faculty and academic leaders?

Peter Ewell, a long-serving board member and an internationally respected expert on the assessment of student learning, provides answers to these and other important questions in *Making the Grade: How Boards Can Ensure Academic Quality*. First published in 2006 and soon known broadly by boards, faculty, provosts, and assessment specialists as "the little yellow book," *Making the Grade* is now in its second edition, complete with a new introduction and a new description of the backdrop against which higher education boards now work. New references to online and print resources add to the value of the book.

Written by a board member for board members, this very readable book makes a compelling case for greater board engagement in discussions of student learning and educational quality. As Ewell asserts, "Ensuring academic quality is a fiduciary responsibility; it is as much a part of our role as board members as ensuring that the institution has sufficient resources and is spending them wisely." In addition to bringing clarity to board responsibilities in overseeing quality, *Making the Grade* provides excellent guidance for academic affairs committees. The questions found at the end of each chapter can help shape fruitful discussion by boards and committees.

This second edition of *Making the Grade: How Boards Can Ensure Academic Quality* continues the important conversation begun by the original publication in 2006, and it sharpens the focus on the need for higher education to make progress in assessing and improving student learning.

This book is part of a group of AGB publications that help boards undertake this critical part of their fiduciary responsibilities effectively. In addition to AGB's 2010 report on "How Boards Oversee Educational Quality," there is AGB's Effective Committee Series which includes *The Academic Affairs Committee* and Richard Morrill's groundbreaking book, *Strategic Leadership in Academic Affairs* (2002), which provides a big-picture look at boards and the educational enterprise.

AGB's 2011 statement on "Board Responsibility for Overseeing Educational Quality" provides guiding principles for boards, provosts, and presidents. It is included in its entirety in the Appendix of this edition.

Finally, AGB is appreciative of the significant contributions Peter Ewell has made to the quality of higher education governance through his thoughtful, authoritative, and sensible writing on the essential topic of board oversight of academic quality.

Susan Whealler Johnston

Executive Vice President and Chief Operating Officer
Association of Governing Boards of Universities and Colleges
December 2012

INTRODUCTION

A s board members, we are accustomed to looking after the financial health and fiscal integrity of our institutions. Virtually every board meeting we attend features reviews of budgets, revenue projections, capital needs, or the approval of specific expenditures. Many of us also sit on the foundation boards of our institutions, where examining specific investments and associated returns is the principal order of business. But at many institutions, the board only rarely gets to look directly at the heart of the academic enterprise: the quality of teaching and learning. This is confirmed by the results of AGB's recent survey of board members and academic administrators, which indicates that almost two-thirds of respondents do not feel that enough time is spent examining student learning at board meetings.[1]

For many reasons, this state of affairs has begun to change—and change it should. As in the far-more-visible world of elementary and secondary education, the products of our colleges and universities are experiencing intensive public scrutiny because of the overwhelming importance of developing the nation's "educational capital" in a globally competitive world. At the same time, competition within higher education for more and better students means that attention to academic quality must be paramount if the institutions for which we are responsible are to prosper.

As in other realms of institutional operations, it is up to the faculty and administration to uphold and improve academic quality. But it is up to the board to understand it and to see that it gets done. Ensuring academic quality is a fiduciary responsibility; it is as much part of our role as board members as ensuring that the

---

[1] "How Boards Oversee Educational Quality: A Report on a Survey on Boards and the Assessment of Student Learning" (AGB, 2010).

institution has sufficient resources and is spending them wisely.[2]

Most boards have academic affairs committees that are responsible for broad oversight of the institution's academic functions, including programs, curricula, teaching, research, and faculty affairs. These committees have a specific responsibility for ensuring that academic quality assurance and improvement mechanisms are in place. They can be expected, for example, to look carefully at the evidence about student learning or the results of academic-program review, then engage in interpretive dialogue with senior academic administrators and faculty committee chairs to determine potential implications and what improvements can be made. Occasionally, such dialogue will result in a recommendation to the full board about a potential strategic direction with respect to academic programming or a needed investment. For small boards that have no discrete academic affairs committee, the full board will have to judiciously assume these responsibilities.

My intent in this book is to review the substance of what board members should know about the various dimensions of academic quality, the mechanisms colleges and universities use to investigate and improve it, and the kinds of questions we should ask our presidents and chief academic officers about how the institution is doing. I briefly examine the various changes that have occurred in both the academy and its operating context that now compel attention in ensuring academic quality. I then go on to review four major elements of academic quality assurance and improvement that boards should know about:

1. the assessment of student learning,
2. student retention and graduation rates,
3. stakeholder satisfaction, and
4. academic-program review.

Each is briefly described in terms of how the process works and the kinds of questions board members should ask about results. For each, moreover, I list re-

---

[2] Consistent with Principle 1 of the "AGB Statement on Board Responsibility for the Oversight of Educational Quality" (AGB, 2011): See Appendix, page 109.

sponsibilities particularly appropriate to the academic affairs committee. A final chapter addresses institutional and program accreditation—the increasingly important process of external review that draws upon internal evidence and certifies quality for an institution's many stakeholders.

Defining the Territory

One way to organize the processes that make up academic quality assurance and explain how they fit together is to visualize the institution's teaching and learning functions as they would work in a typical business enterprise. Given this perspective, questions such as the following will be familiar to most boards of directors in other settings:

- **How good is our product?** For colleges and universities, the principal product is student learning, and the quality of learning outcomes should be a central concern. Just as in a manufacturing enterprise, quality needs to be examined from at least two perspectives: the ultimate quality of the product on completion (that is, what a student knows and can do upon graduation) and the "value added" by the "production process" of instruction (that is, how much more a student knows and can do upon graduation than he or she did upon entering the institution). Determining these is the business of *assessment*.

- **How good are we at producing our product?** Like every other "production process," college-level instruction entails a certain amount of "waste." Not all students who enter our institutions as freshmen will complete their programs, and many of those who do will "stop out" for some period of time or will otherwise finish late. Patterns of student flow into and through our institutions are important to monitor because they affect both costs and outcomes. As a result, every institution should know something about *student retention and graduation*.

- **Are our customers satisfied?** Like all businesses, colleges and universities have a range of stakeholders, and the perceptions they maintain about our institutions are important to monitor because they will strongly affect whether the stakeholders continue to relate to and invest in us. Among the key stakeholders from whom we must seek such information are students, their parents, potential students and *their* parents, employers, civic opinion leaders, and members of the public in the regions we serve. Periodically examining *stakeholder perceptions and opinions* can help tailor our product and anticipate emerging needs.

- **Do we have the right "mix" of products?** Like businesses that typically offer diverse "product mixes," colleges and universities offer degrees in many fields and provide instruction at multiple levels. Thus, regardless of the levels of outcomes achieved and the efficiency of the production process, institutions should periodically take stock of their "product portfolios" to determine whether they are offering the right things at the right levels in the light of graduate quality and the marketplace. Stock-taking of this kind is typically a part of *academic program review*.

- **Do we make the grade?** Businesses that want to stay competitive must obtain external certifications or ratings of their quality. For products, that may take the form of a certification by Underwriters Laboratories (UL) or a Good Housekeeping Seal. Companies themselves can pursue international quality certifications such as ISO 9001 or seek the Malcolm Baldrige National Quality Award. For colleges and universities, the basic quality certification is *institutional accreditation*, and it is critical for institutions if they are to remain in good standing.

Analogies between the academy and the world of business, of course, can be overdrawn. But characterizing some of the basic processes of academic management and quality assurance in business language emphasizes the fact that academic affairs should not be considered alien territory by members of the board who do not happen to be academics. Familiar principles of wise management and judicious oversight should inform these functions just as they do any other.

Defining the Board's Role

The basic questions posed here are not only colloquial but are intentionally pitched at a level appropriate for board involvement. The role of the board in academic-quality assurance, as in any other area, needs to be defined in terms of explicit boundary conditions that guard against overstepping the line between exercising necessary fiduciary responsibility for the institution and directly managing its operations. While this is always a delicate balance, it is even more so in academic affairs, where issues tend to be more complex than in more "businesslike" areas of institutional functioning such as finance, personnel management, communications, and fundraising.

Why are academic-quality issues more complex? Partly because faculty from different disciplines often have different values with respect to what is most important in the curriculum and what constitutes high-quality performance. Thus there is much more ambiguity than in whether a fiscal bottom line is black or red. Lines of authority, too, are less clear-cut: Academic matters typically are managed by consensus, and individual faculty and departments are legitimately accorded a great deal of autonomy in defining what they do with respect to instruction and how they do it. These factors mean that coming to agreement and closure on academic matters may take a good deal of time.

This state of affairs means that boards need to display patience in allowing the process of academic deliberation to run its course. But it also means that board members should continue to press for answers and avoid the temptation to stop asking questions just because the process seems stalled.

One way to achieve clarity about the board's proper role in these matters is to consider the following principles:

- **Running the curriculum is the faculty's responsibility; the board's role is to remind them of that responsibility.** Principles of shared governance at any institution mean that primary responsibility for an academic program is vested in its faculty. This means that faculty first must define the learning outcomes that students are expected to achieve in each academic program and

The Academic Affairs Committee

For boards that have an academic affairs committee, dialogues about academic quality should be deeper, but the need to maintain appropriate balance becomes even more important.

Academic affairs committees are expected to examine evidence of academic quality in greater detail than the full board, as well as discuss emerging implications with academic leaders and senior faculty members. Such discussions may well raise questions about curricular change, program inventory, the need for greater attention to faculty development, and potentially significant investments in instructional technology. Because of their unique position and ability to see the issues from the point of view of the institution as a whole, rather than from the perspective of a particular department or school, committee members may be able to shed a different interpretive light on some of this evidence and should not hesitate to do so. But like the full board, committee members should be mindful that their role is about strategic direction, not the details of how things should be done.

for the institution as a whole, then design and deliver a curriculum consistent with these objectives.

Although some variance in how each faculty member teaches toward established learning objectives is normal, it is both appropriate and important for the board to insist that all faculty members *have* such objectives, that instructors are conscious about designing learning activities consistent with those objectives, and that they are collecting evidence that those objectives are being attained. It is also important for the board to remind faculty members that such work is an integral part of their academic responsibility. But it is beyond the board's appropriate role to question or dictate the *content* of those intended outcomes, or the particular instructional designs and approaches used to achieve them.

- **Stay focused on strategic issues.** Strategic issues are "mission-critical"—that is, they are issues that, if left unattended, will threaten the institution's ability to fulfill its purposes. Balanced budgets, for example, are mission-critical, which is why boards pay so much attention to achieving them. But all of the business-oriented questions noted earlier are mission-critical, too. Student retention, for example, is mission-critical because it affects not only tuition revenue but also institutional reputation, which is essential for attracting new students. Program mix is mission-critical because it matters greatly to the student markets that an institution wants to tap, and because it largely characterizes institutional type and aspirations. And maintaining the quality of student-learning outcomes is mission-critical because those outcomes are used to validate the claims that an institution makes about its graduates—claims that, if unsubstantiated, will affect graduates' employment and post-graduate opportunities and ultimately an institution's ability to attract new students.

In this regard, strategic questions should reflect how well the institution is performing its fundamental job of graduating students who are competent and well prepared. They should *not* address the specific changes needed in response to negative assessment results. Similarly, strategic questions may reflect new opportunities for institutional markets or reveal the potential need for new programs during a program review. They are *not* about designing the content or dictating the instructional approaches of new programs.

- **Expect and demand a culture of evidence.** In the past, colleges and universities viewed academic quality as intangible, impossible to measure, and dependent on the eye of the beholder. That traditional view rested largely on institutional resources and reputation as a proxy for academic quality.

  The current premise of academic-quality assurance, however, takes an entirely opposite view, holding that it *is* possible to assemble meaningful and generalizable evidence of academic quality and to act on that data to improve teaching and learning. But because many of the processes in place to do so are new and unfamiliar, there remains a tendency at many institutions to make assertions about student learning or program quality based largely on anecdote.

  Boards should not let that happen. Conversations about academic quality in any of its dimensions should be based on *evidence*. Boards should insist on it, and administrators and faculty members should come to expect it. Whenever claims about quality, effectiveness, or improvement are made, boards should always ask, "How do we know that?" If evidence-based answers are not offered, the follow-up question should be, "What would it take to find out?"

In many cases, adequate evidence may not be available for legitimate reasons: Methodologies for gathering appropriate evidence in some areas may be unavailable, inapplicable to the institution's circumstances, or simply too expensive to pursue in a cost-effective way. But the board nevertheless has a responsibility to ask the right questions.

- **Recognize that evidence about academic quality raises issues but rarely gives final answers.** Much of the evidence generated by academic-quality reviews ends up being presented in numeric form and, as a result, has an air of precision that suggests finality. In truth, though, such data usually represents not the end but rather the beginning of a conversation. This will be the case particularly in the deliberations of the academic affairs committee, where evidence about academic quality should be regularly presented and thoroughly discussed. Such conversations are not exclusively confined to the academic affairs committee, however. Accordingly, when presented with such data, both board and committee members should not just take them at face value but should instead ask administrators what *they* think the data mean and what action implications grow out of the findings.

When reviewing academic-quality data, committee members should also be aware that such statistics mean little without an interpretive context. One way of providing context is to establish a point of comparison. So committee members might ask how a given statistic about academic performance compares with the same information from the previous year, or with similar figures nationally, or with comparable data from peer institutions. Another way to provide context is by breaking down the statistics further to examine what they reveal about different campus populations or programs. So the committee might, for example, ask how men performed in comparison with women, how particular academic programs fared in comparison with one another, or how students receiving institutional aid performed.

Finally, because academic quality is complex and elusive, no single piece of evidence tells the whole story. Committee members instead should ask administrators to provide evidence drawn from multiple sources and to engage the campus in holistic conversation about the "big picture" that emerges from a presented body of evidence.

> **66** No single piece of evidence tells the whole story. **99**

- **Make reviewing evidence of academic quality and improvement a regular and expected board-level activity.** Considered in the context of pressing board business—such as approving budgets, looking at construction progress reports, and handling legal matters—it is easy to put off looking at academics. Yet teaching and learning constitutes every institution's main business, and academic quality should be of paramount concern to the board. Because the faculty and administration bear most of this responsibility, the board's overall level of engagement in this area need not be time-consuming, but it does need to be systematic.

Reviewing the results of all four sources of evidence of academic quality—the assessment of student learning, student retention and graduation rates, stakeholder satisfaction, and academic-program review—should be the explicit responsibility of the academic affairs committee, which should establish a regular schedule for doing so in collaboration with academic leadership.

Meanwhile, regular opportunities for academic-quality review should be built into the board's annual work plan—whether by scheduling annual reviews of "dashboard" performance indicators containing data on academic quality, making discussions about quality an integral part of a strategic-planning exercise, or making assessment results a topic for a board retreat where more in-depth conversations can occur. Finally, the full board should be aware of preparations for institutional accreditation—a process that today focuses more heavily on the assessment of student-learning outcomes—and should thoroughly discuss the resulting accreditation report with administrators to determine what should be done in response.

The bottom line is that knowledge about the academic condition of the enterprise is as critical for a board as knowledge about the institution's fiscal condition. As Derek Bok, a professor of law and president emeritus of Harvard University, wrote in a 2005 essay in the *Chronicle of Higher Education*: "The traditional roles of trustees are *both* to defend and promote the interests of their institutions *and* to represent the concerns and needs of the public that does much to subsidize and sustain higher education. Examining the methods used to enhance the quality of education is a natural way of discharging the second role."[3]

Yet it is important to keep the board's involvement *strategic* by (1) ensuring that the right kinds of academic quality-assurance processes are in place and (2) periodically asking questions about how the administration is using the information it collects about the academic effectiveness to improve teaching and learning.[4]

To reiterate, the board has a fiduciary responsibility to ensure that the institution is meeting its obligations. In this regard, a favorable accreditation outcome is as important to an institution as a clean financial audit. The board also must be assured that the administration is effectively managing the institution and is using tools and approaches consistent with known best practices in academic management—including learning assessment, monitoring student flow, soliciting feedback from students and stakeholders, and regularly reviewing the quality of academic programs.

The full board and/or its academic affairs committee ensures that these im-

---

[3] Bok, Derek, "The Critical Role of Trustees in Enhancing Student Learning," *Chronicle of Higher Education*, December 16, 2005.

[4] Consistent with Principle 2 of the "AGB Statement on Board Responsibility for the Oversight of Educational Quality" (AGB, 2011): See Appendix, page 110.

portant processes are in place and functioning effectively by requiring annual reports from the president and chief academic officer on the institution's results and any consequent issues of academic quality. It is as important for the board to know that the right mechanisms are in place and being utilized as it is for the board to know that the institution is following sound budgeting and accounting practices.

Finally, as in any corporation, the board has ultimate responsibility for the soundness of the institution's products and the integrity of its operations. Ultimately, that means that the board must be able to stand behind the competitiveness of its institution's graduates with respect to their knowledge and skills and to the academic integrity of the curriculum that prepared them. This is what we signify when we stand with our faculty and graduates at every commencement convocation. We need to act on this testimony in the boardroom as well.

> **" Ultimately, the board must be able to stand behind the competitiveness of its institution's graduates...their knowledge and skills and the academic integrity of the curriculum that prepared them. "**

A RISING INTEREST
IN ACADEMIC QUALITY

For many years, judgments about "quality" in higher education were de-termined almost solely by institutional reputation, productivity, and fac-tors such as fiscal, physical, and human resources. Publicly funded insti-tutions, for example, routinely reported on the preparation levels of the students they admitted, as well as unit costs in relation to enrollments and student credit hours. Regional accreditors, charged with examining the adequacy of public and independent institutions alike, looked mostly at the overall level of institutional resources and at internal shared-governance processes. Where each of these re-porting processes touched the realm of academic affairs, it was largely to examine curricular structures and faculty credentials.

Over the past three decades, however, interest on the part of external stake-holders in the actual academic performance of colleges and universities has steadily risen. There are a number of reasons for the increased concern:

- a growing atmosphere of *accountability* in higher education, with an empha-sis on student-learning outcomes;
- increased *competition* in the higher education marketplace, an environment that puts a premium on visible evidence of academic performance; and
- the constrained fiscal conditions under which most colleges and universities operate today—a context that puts a premium on sound and *evidence-based academic management* practices as much as it does on fiscal discipline.

■ THE BASICS

Rising Calls for Accountability

Beginning in the mid-1980s, state policy makers grew concerned about the outcomes of higher education in relation to its costs. Educational quality already was on the minds of governors and state legislators because of the Reagan administration's "A Nation at Risk" report in 1983, which warned of declining learning standards in elementary and secondary schools. In that climate, the National Governors Association launched an initiative in 1985 titled "Time for Results," extending a call to examine the quality of collegiate learning—a call that continues to reverberate today.

A key result of those changes was the birth of a nationwide assessment movement in higher education that has stimulated the development of systematic investigations of student-learning outcomes at growing numbers of colleges and universities. Although the states were at first the main drivers of that effort, the push to remain internationally competitive has lately driven the federal government, acting through regional accrediting organizations, to step up engagement with quality and pay greater attention to improving graduation rates in higher education.

In the early 2000s, the rising interest in the quality of higher education was joined by a growing national imperative, fueled by a concern that the United States was no longer unquestionably the world leader in higher education. According to figures compiled by the Organisation for Economic Cooperation and Development (OECD), the U.S. slipped to 15th place in the world with respect to the proportion of young citizens (aged 25-34) earning a postsecondary credential.[5] And both the Bush and Obama administrations expressed support for the creation of a "unit record" database to let the government track college graduates and gather data about job placement and career success—and, by extension, about which institutions produce the most successful graduates.

---

[5] Organisation for Economic Cooperation and Development, "Education at a Glance 2011," Paris: Organisation for Economic Co-operation and Development, 2011.

Clearly, improving the quality of learning outcomes, through reforming remedial education and other means, is integral to achieving the United States' goals. Operating in a global environment means that the nation needs to maintain competitiveness with respect to both the numbers and the quality of degrees produced.

The Role of the States

The explicit interest of states in higher education quality embraces more than just public institutions, and it is driven by three factors:

- First, state governments are "owner-operators" of public colleges and universities, which they directly fund and oversee. As such, state policy makers are fundamentally interested in *cost-effectiveness and return on investment*. With respect to outcomes, that means that policy makers want to be assured that graduates have reached acceptable levels of academic performance in relation to the state's costs. But they are also concerned about such matters as student retention and the time it takes students to earn their degrees because those factors are assumed to be related to efficiency as well.

- Second, many states provide substantial scholarship support that allows students to attend independent as well as public institutions. Acting in this role, a state's primary concern with respect to academic-quality assurance is that students obtain a credential of *value*—that is, one with which graduates are satisfied and that has a payoff in the marketplace for employment.

- Finally, in their roles as keepers of *the public interest*, states are concerned about issues including economic development, civic participation, and the overall quality of life of their citizens. Accordingly, they are interested in related dimensions of quality in higher education, such as college and university contributions to economic development in the form of well-prepared graduates, contributions to knowledge consistent with state needs, and institutional responsiveness to regional and community needs. These elements of quality, of course, can be manifest in both public and independent institutions.

While these basic interests in academic accountability are common across the 50 states, they may differ in their expression. For example, a few states require students at public institutions to pass standardized examinations and/or participate in statewide surveys about what they learned and experienced. But far more states require public institutions to report regularly on student outcomes using institution-defined criteria and assessment methods. And almost all states include graduation-rate data as part of their performance-indicator systems for public higher education. Some states are even beginning to include independent institutions in these reports as well, using data on student progress collected through those institutions' participation in state-funded student-aid programs.

Institutional Accreditation

Increasingly, though, institutional accrediting organizations are displacing states as the primary actors in quality assurance for higher education. Accreditation is a nominally voluntary process that began about a century ago as a means for colleges and universities to recognize and accept one another's credits and credentials. To remain accredited, institutions go through a comprehensive review process every five to eight years that involves preparation of a self-study, one or more multi-day visits by a team of peer reviewers, and a review-and-report process noting institutional strengths and areas for improvement together with a judgment regarding the institution's continuing accreditation status. (*See Chapter 6.*)

The "teeth" in accreditation lies in the fact that institutions must remain accredited to continue to participate in the U.S. Education Department's extensive financial-aid programs, which include both need-based aid and low-interest student loans. Most colleges and universities participate heavily in both programs, which provide institutions with a significant component of tuition revenue. This link between accreditation and federal funds exists because the federal government has essentially deputized accrediting organizations to review institutional quality on its behalf, in lieu of creating an extensive and expensive federal accountability process for higher education.

In order to ensure that they are doing what the federal government wants, accrediting organizations are themselves periodically reviewed by the Education Department and officially recognized as gatekeepers for federal funds. And since about 1990, one of the most prominent conditions for continuing recognition is a requirement that accrediting organizations emphasize the assessment of student learning in their reviews of institutions. The result has been increased attention to learning outcomes by accrediting teams when they visit campuses. This greater emphasis is one of the most important reasons why board members should be aware of their institution's activities in assessing student-learning outcomes and of how faculty and staff are using assessment results to improve teaching and learning.

Although accountability demands on colleges and universities have increased markedly over the past decade, there is mounting evidence that those demands will only increase. Beginning in 2007, the U.S. Department of Education began putting increased pressure on recognized accreditors to more rigorously examine institutions on the quality of their learning outcomes. That pressure came in the wake of recommendations by the Secretary's Commission on the Future of Higher Education (commonly known as the "Spellings Commission"), issued in 2006. While the Commission stopped short of suggesting that the federal government require accreditors to use standardized tests of student-learning outcomes, the Commission did urge institutions to adopt such testing programs that would allow the competitive performance of their graduates to be determined and urged accreditors to require such testing. As a result, more and more, accreditors will look not only at the adequacy of an institution's assessment efforts, but also at what those assessments reveal about the levels of learning being achieved, and for satisfactory performance against available benchmarks.

These developments are harbingers of an institutional operating environment in which accountability for academic quality is playing an ever larger part. Board members need to know about the growing salience of accountability as a driver of demands for evidence of academic quality in order to ensure that their institutions are in a position to respond.

Increased Competition in the Higher Ed Marketplace

For most public institutions, state funding has become a steadily diminishing share of revenues. Public institutions have been compensating for the shortfalls by raising tuition—a tactic that most independent institutions also depend on to sustain their revenues. This state of affairs means that maintaining enrollment is a critical concern for all colleges and universities today.

But most institutions are not interested in simply "maintaining enrollment"—rather, they want to recruit and attract a specific kind of student body. That desire has fostered an increasingly competitive environment, as growing numbers of public and independent institutions try to attract the best (or most suitable) students available in their recruitment pools, as well as those willing and able to pay the full cost of tuition. Indeed, for many institutions, the traditional distinctions between public and independent have disappeared. Both tend to recruit from the same markets, and both increasingly use mechanisms such as institutional aid to shape their enrollments.

The Pros and Cons of Rankings

Operating in such a market-oriented environment increasingly requires an understanding of academic quality, since evidence of quality can be a valuable tool in enhancing an institution's competitiveness. Perhaps most emblematic of this fact is the current dominance of the rankings published each fall by *U.S. News & World Report* in a feature titled "America's Best Colleges."

The *U.S. News* rankings have been issued for almost three decades and are firmly established in the higher education landscape. But the actual role of the rankings—and perhaps more importantly, our attitudes toward them—are contradictory. The evidence is slim that the *U.S. News* rankings actually influence student choice very much,[6] yet their symbolic value has become enormous.

Institutional leaders rightly want to maintain their standing in *U.S. News*

---

[6] McDonough, Patricia M.; Anthony Lising Antonio; Mary Beth Walpole; and Leonor Perez. *College Rankings: Who Uses Them and with What Impact?* Los Angeles: Graduate School of Education and Information Studies, University of California at Los Angeles, 1997.

rankings, even as they criticize the way the rankings are constructed and decry them as an invalid measure of quality. Board members, too, need to understand that the rankings are flawed, and should not become upset if the institution slips a few notches in the rankings. But they also need to understand that some of the statistical ingredients of the rankings—and some alternatives to them—*do* warrant monitoring to help shape the institution's enrollment-management strategies.

- One such ingredient is *the quality of entering students*—a characteristic captured, to some extent, by the *U.S. News* rankings in the form of the percentage of applicants admitted. Many institutions have goals that address the quality of their incoming class, so looking at this factor over time to determine if standards are being maintained is worthy of leadership's attention. This statistic is flawed as a management indicator, however, because many institutions have a limited pool of potential candidates that are attracted to them for their distinctive characteristics. Such institutions thus tend to select a high proportion of applicants from this limited group, which usually includes adequate numbers of superior students.

  Therefore, in addition to examining information on the size and shape of the admissions pool and the percentage and number of applicants admitted, the board should also be aware of the admissions "yield"—the percentage admitted who actually enroll. Similarly, if the institution is fairly selective, it also will be important to look at the quality of the incoming class in terms of such standard indicators as high-school class rank, SAT or ACT scores, and any special characteristics that students may exhibit.

- A second important dimension of performance captured in part by the *U.S. News* rankings is *the rate at which students complete their degrees*. Graduation-rate reporting is a prominent element of accountability, and the federal government has, since 1989, required all institutions to calculate those data using a standard methodology and make the statistics available to potential students and their parents. (*See Chapter 3.*) Information on graduations rates is important for institutions, too, for use in their strategic enrollment planning and recruitment efforts.

For their part, board members need to understand that graduation rates correlate highly with the academic ability of an incoming class, and that increased selectivity almost always will result in increased retention. Boards also need to understand that retaining students of middling ability is a more efficient way to maintain enrollments (and therefore revenue) than simply admitting more new freshmen who then drop out. These financial entailments of recruitment and retention are not always apparent, though they are important institutional strategies.

Still, the *U.S. News* rankings are rightly criticized for capturing few authentic dimensions of academic quality. In fact, recent research has demonstrated that, overall, they have almost no relationship to the kinds of high-quality academic experiences associated with substantial learning gain.

> **" Board members should be aware that alternative measures of institutional quality exist. "**

This disparity has led to a number of efforts to develop alternative measures of institutional quality that focus more strongly on such experiences. The National Survey of Student Engagement (NSSE), for example, was developed in the late 1990s for exactly that purpose. A few years later, the NSSE was joined by a counterpart for two-year colleges, the Community College Survey of Student Engagement (CCSSE). The surveys ask students to report on their own behaviors, as well as on teaching and learning practices and other aspects of the institution's instructional environment that empirical research has shown to be significantly related to learning.

Board members should be aware that these alternative measures of institutional quality exist and might better characterize their institution's mission and the educational setting it is trying to market. In fact, in some notable cases, institutions using NSSE have, as part of their marketing efforts, posted their results either as a supplement or an alternative to the *U.S. News* rankings.

A Shift Toward Evidence-Based Management

A final factor stimulating the focus on academic quality has been the rise of new approaches to managing the curriculum and the teaching and learning processes. In adopting such techniques—derived, in part, from corporate practices—colleges and universities have been responding both to increased competitiveness and the fact that they have found that better management of academic resources can help them achieve more on a fixed-resource base without sacrificing quality.

Institutions originally worked to improve their information resources to generate the statistics needed to respond to growing accountability demands. But much of the attraction of developing even more powerful information resources came from a different source: evidence-based management techniques, such as Total Quality Management (TQM) and Continuous Quality Improvement (CQI), which emerged in business and manufacturing in the 1990s.

Many board members who work in the business and professional community are familiar with techniques like TQM and CQI and, more important, with the principles of evidence-based management that lie behind them. Where appropriate, those board members should ask administrators if and how they apply such principles.

Colleges and universities first began applying quality-management techniques drawn from business to tasks in areas where they seemed most suitable, such as operations and maintenance of the physical plant, personnel management, financial services, and procurement. Among the most commonly used techniques were "mapping" standardized processes (such as cutting a reimbursement check) for the purpose of streamlining them, statistical process control (in such areas as purchasing) to ensure reliable consistent service, and outsourcing such functions as food services and computing.

More recently, however, some of those same techniques have been fruitfully applied to processes related to teaching and learning by focusing on achieving a better understanding of the academic "production function"—that is, how students flow through a set of courses in a particular curriculum, what they experience, and the outcomes they achieve. Of particular importance is improving course sequencing so that students are immediately able to apply what they have learned in the appropriate settings. The effectiveness of those connections can then be monitored by looking at how students perform in subsequent sequential courses in relation to what they experienced and how they performed in previous (prerequisite) courses in the same sequence. Such techniques have enabled much more effective and coherent learning experiences, and have proved to be especially applicable in fields such as mathematics and in remedial coursework, in which it is possible to specify and teach to concrete learning outcomes. They also have proved especially important in the growing arena of technology-mediated instructional delivery.

Colleges and universities are, further, using the principles of evidence-based management to make decisions about the overall shape of the institution's academic offerings—that is, what kinds of programs to offer in what fields and at what levels. Increasingly, such decisions are based in part on careful market research and needs analysis to determine the nature and extent of demand and to establish pricing policies. At the same time, analysis of current patterns of enrollment, retention and completion, assessment results, and job or graduate-school placement data can reveal whether the institution's current array of programs is optimal. Those analyses may then, in turn, lead to evidence-based decisions about whether to expand capacity in a given program, scale it back, or eliminate it altogether. While such decisions are the kinds that academic administrators have always had to make, the difference now is that those decisions increasingly are based on concrete evidence, using a growing array of indicators of program need and performance.

It is important for board members to recognize that there are, of course, limits to the applicability of quality-management techniques in academic settings. Teaching and learning are not the same as making widgets. And just because board members are familiar with quality-management applications in business settings does not mean that they can commend them to academic leaders without qualification. At the same time, it is important for academic leaders to become aware of the appropriate potential applications of quality-management principles, and the board's questions may be a good stimulus.

> **" Colleges can no more do without a systematic program of student-outcomes assessment than they could do without a development office. "**

In sum, these three conditions of doing business in the new academy—escalating accountability demands, increased competitiveness in the market for students, and the development of evidence-based management techniques to help deal with fiscal realities—together point to a growing need for new kinds of information about academic quality. Board members should realize that these conditions are not going to recede anytime soon, but instead have quickly become permanent features of the higher education landscape that are shaping institutional behavior in important ways. Consequently, boards need to advocate for having the right kinds of evidence-gathering and quality-management systems in place in the realm of teaching and learning as much as they now advocate for new sources of revenues and greater operating efficiencies in the institution's nonacademic functions.

In short, to succeed in this new reality, colleges and universities can no more do without a systematic program of student-outcomes assessment than they could do without a development office.

ASSESSING STUDENT-LEARNING OUTCOMES

Many board members may be surprised to learn that systematic investigations of what students know and can do as a result of attending a college or university have emerged only in the past 25 years at most American institutions. Unlike our counterparts in the United Kingdom and elsewhere in the English-speaking world, colleges and universities in the United States do not employ external examiners to provide an outside check on student academic performance. Nor do we have national subject examinations as do many European countries such as France and Germany.

Instead, the American approach to delivering an undergraduate curriculum has traditionally given individual faculty members the authority to run their courses as they see fit, awarding standard letter grades to certify student performance. Passing the requisite numbers, types, and levels of courses in this manner in most cases fulfills the requirements for a baccalaureate degree (though many institutions now also require "capstone" courses, or exercises at the end of a student's program). Thus, all that is typically known about a typical student's *overall* performance in college is how many credits he or she has completed, as well as a grade-point average calculated on the basis of his or her grades, as awarded by 40 or so individual faculty members.

As long as few questions were asked about the quality of graduates' overall learning, such an approach seemed acceptable. But when those questions did begin to surface in the early 1980s, grades alone no longer sufficed.

■ THE BASICS

Why Grades Aren't Enough

Because it is common for the topic of grades to come up during discussions of how to assess student-learning outcomes, board members ought to know *why* grades alone no longer suffice as proof of learning, and why the subject of grades has become controversial. Arguments against the usefulness of grades as a measure of learning generally include the following points:

- Even if one assumes that faculty-awarded grades are valid and consistent, they still address only the domain of a particular class and its specific content.

- Because an instructor may take a student's generic abilities (such as writing) into account when awarding grades, there is no way to know how much weight any two faculty members assign to such abilities in the grading process.

- Even if it is clear exactly *what* all faculty are assessing when they grade, and the weight they give to each sub-ability, there is no assurance of consistency across the *standards* they use for grading.

- Grades generally are awarded on a curve, with a given proportion of students expected for each possible grade—a practice that can conceal the possibility that few or no students in the class actually met the professor's previously established standard.

- Perhaps most important, the distribution of grades awarded in a given class indicates nothing about the patterns of strengths and weaknesses of the class as a whole with respect to learning— information that, if available, could be used to make improvements.

Assessment of student learning has thus become an imperative for higher education as better answers to the above concerns have become increasingly important, both for reasons of accountability and for reasons of academic improvement.

Academic assessment comprises a set of systematic methods for collecting valid and reliable evidence of what students *know* and *can do* at various stages in their academic careers—distinct accomplishments that break down as follows:

- *What a student knows* refers to the familiar *cognitive dimension* of learned concepts or disciplinary content (for example, a biological taxonomy, the principles of accounting, or the writings of the major Victorian poets).

- *What a student can do* refers to the *performance dimension* of learning, most frequently manifested in the form of a demonstrable skill (for example, the ability to write a succinct paragraph that critiques an argument, to design and carry out a physics experiment, or to debug a computer program).

Occasionally, "affective" or "attitudinal" dimensions are added to the list of intended learning outcomes—for example, ethical behavior, an ability to operate in a diverse or global environment, or a sense of personal responsibility. Assessment may mean gathering evidence about any of those attributes, and may be undertaken at the disciplinary or major-program level, for an institution's general education program, or for an institution as a whole (though most institutions will conduct all three kinds of assessments).

> 66 Occasionally, 'attitudinal' dimensions are added to the list of intended learning outcomes: ethical behavior, ability to operate in a diverse or global environment... personal responsibility. 99

Statements of Learning Outcomes

Any assessment is governed by formal statements of "intended learning outcomes" that are developed by a program's faculty or by representative faculty and staff members for the institution as a whole. For employment-related programs, or for programs with specialized accreditation, such statements are frequently developed in consultation with employers or professional associations. For more traditional academic disciplines, such as psychology and political science, national disciplinary associations are increasingly developing model sets of program-level student-learning outcomes that faculty can use as guides.

To establish statements of more general student-learning outcomes—those expected of all of the institution's graduates, for example—a frequent starting point is the mission statement, which generally sets forth the qualities the institution seeks to instill in its graduates. But the language contained in most mission statements illustrates the challenge of constructing meaningful statements of intended learning outcomes: Such language is often so vague and general that it provides little guidance for gathering evidence.

Strong learning-outcomes statements, in contrast, are cast in active language (e.g., "Graduates safely handle chemical materials, taking into account their physical and chemical properties, including any specific hazards associated with their use"), and are sufficiently concrete to enable an actual task or demonstration to be constructed (e.g., "Graduates can summarize and explain the findings of an empirical study in sociology, including a critical assessment of the methodological frameworks used").

Ultimately, academic-assessment programs are designed primarily to collect information about student performance in the *aggregate* in order to ground judgments about overall program quality or to uncover general strengths and weaknesses that can be used as the basis for further program development. Their primary purpose is to draw general conclusions about teaching and learning, not about individual people. That distinction is what makes academic-assessment programs different from certification programs that govern entry into a profession, such as state bar exams or medical licensing procedures: Evidence from licensure or certification may be used in institutional assessment, but the intent is to analyze and disaggregate such evidence to learn something about how the *program* is functioning, not just to count the number of individuals who passed. The fact that the unit of analysis is collective instead of individual also means that the evaluator need not assess all students. In many cases, samples of student work or performance are used because they may be adequate to draw valid conclusions.

The Difference Between Higher Education Assessments and K-12 Assessments

Because many board members may be more familiar with the assessment procedures currently used in elementary and secondary education than with those in collegiate settings, a few words about the differences are in order.

Under the federal No Child Left Behind law, all elementary school children in certain grades must be tested using standardized achievement examinations developed by each state. Schools are compared based on their students' performance on the examinations, and low-performing schools are sanctioned. Although much criticized, these procedures are in part justifiable because all schoolchildren are supposed to learn the same things at the same levels, regardless of where they go to school. Furthermore, the knowledge and skills in question are relatively easy to test.

Higher education differs from this (to many, more familiar) school context in at least two ways:

1. **Colleges differ widely with respect to mission, so it is legitimate to expect differences in the learning outcomes they seek to foster in their students.** As a result, institution-based efforts to assess student-learning outcomes vary from place to place with respect both to the outcomes that institutions examine and the kinds of evidence that they use in the process.

2. **At the collegiate level, higher-order learning outcomes are complex and therefore difficult to measure.** As a result, although standardized-test results are sometimes used, so is a wide range of other evidence, including essays, specially designed assignments, projects, demonstrations, and portfolios. There is a good deal of appropriate variety across colleges and universities with respect to the shape of their assessment programs, so boards should not expect much standardization. What they should expect, and ensure, is that the methods used and the outcomes assessed are consistent with the institution's mission and values.

QUESTIONS FOR BOARDS TO CONSIDER

Because assessment is so deeply rooted in and driven by the curriculum, it is chiefly a faculty concern. Faculty need to fully own the learning outcomes used to drive the assessment process and should be the primary actors involved in developing them. But the board should become broadly familiar with the basic features of the academic-assessment program and ask judicious questions about it.[7] And members of the academic affairs committee should expect to see and discuss assessment results with academic leaders and faculty committee chairs on a regular basis.

The key questions boards need to ask about assessment are:

1. *Do we clearly state what and how much students should learn? Where do we state it?*

Institutions that seek to earn accreditation today are required to develop and state formal learning-outcomes statements for each academic program or department, as well as for general education (or the degree as a whole). Yet it is surprising how many institutions are not yet in compliance with this requirement, especially at the program level. Boards should (1) ensure that their institutions meet this most basic requirement and (2) be assertive about directing institutional leadership to address the situation promptly if such formal statements do not yet exist.

Boards should also ensure that their institutions' statements of learning outcomes not only describe the desired abilities in question, but also provide some guidance about the *level* at which those abilities should be demonstrated. This kind of specificity would improve many existing statements that currently provide little guidance—either in their configuration or in the kinds of assessment evidence that they require—about how good is good enough.

Finally, board members should be aware that often only a few individuals were involved in developing their institution's existing learning-outcomes statements, and they did so largely just to meet basic accreditation requirements. In such cases, those statements are rarely part of the academic fabric of the institution: They were never internalized by faculty members as collective goals for teaching, nor were they used systematically to inform instructional development and grading.

---

[7] Consistent with Principle 3 of the "AGB Statement on Board Responsibility for the Oversight of Educational Quality" (AGB, 2011): See Appendix, page 111.

But accrediting organizations increasingly are looking for deeper "cultures of evidence," in which goals for learning are widely shared and discussed among faculty members. Accreditors are, furthermore, getting steadily better at determining whether such cultures are present. For example, some accreditors are using techniques such as the European "academic audit," in which two or three academic departments at an institution are selected at random for a "drill-down" review to see how processes such as assessment actually work in practice. Boards should ask academic administrators about the institution's current preparedness to answer such questions. If they were to be audited today, what proportion of departments and faculty would report appropriately?

> 66 Including learning outcomes in syllabi provides an opportunity for faculty to let students know *why* they are being asked to do certain things. 99

Because they are intended to be used as guides for curriculum development and to establish standards against which to judge learning, statements of intended learning outcomes should be made available to, and provide direction for, all faculty members—not serve as mere pro-forma additions to the institution's publications. Equally important, learning-outcomes statements should also be accessible to students via catalogues, course descriptions, and syllabi.

Of those three mediums, syllabi are perhaps most important for establishing intended outcomes: Students learn best when they are aware of the concrete expectations in terms of which their performances on tests and assignments will be judged. Including learning outcomes in syllabi also provides an opportunity for faculty members to let students know *why* they are being asked to do certain things in a given class or learning experience. Too often, students see course requirements as arbitrary and lacking any strong connection to an overarching goal. By showing them a clear path of development and explaining the reasons why certain things are being asked of them, colleges and universities can help students overcome the all-too-typical lack of motivation that many exhibit when they believe learning activities or assignments are irrelevant to their personal situations or goals.

Finally, statements of intended learning outcomes can help focus and differentiate an institution's marketing and student-recruitment efforts. Every institution tries to be distinctive in the message it sends to potential students, stakeholders, and donors. Among the most crucial areas of distinction are the claims it makes about what its graduates know and can do. The more precise and compelling an institution can be when describing its graduates' attributes—and the more persuasive it can be in deploying evidence of their achievements—the more advantage it will have in the marketplace. This will be especially true in the future as employers and graduate programs increasingly seek concrete evidence of student achievement beyond grade-point averages.

In short, boards should ensure that learning-outcomes statements are in place, readily accessible by all campus constituents, and thoughtfully developed for the use and benefit of faculty, administrators, students, and potential students (not to mention the satisfaction of increasingly focused accrediting bodies). Equally or more importantly, boards should also ask whether the goals established are consistent with the institution's mission—that is, do they communicate the distinctive abilities and values for which the institution stands? Such questions do not abrogate faculty prerogative. Instead, they lie at the heart of the board's important role of ensuring the institution's basic purposes.

2. *What kinds of evidence do we collect about learning?*

Board members, and particularly those serving on academic affairs committees, also need to be broadly familiar with the kinds of assessment processes their institutions use to gather or assemble evidence that learning outcomes are being achieved. Board members can most efficiently accomplish this by regularly reviewing their institution's *assessment plan* or schedule (often developed in concert with an established system of program review).

An assessment plan is important for another reason, too: It is one of the first things that a visiting accreditation team will want to see, and after reviewing it, the team may then wish to "drill down" to the level of individual programs and interview faculty members to determine if the plan is real. Given that possibility, it

The Degree Qualifications Profile

In 2011, the Lumina Foundation issued a model set of institutional learning-outcomes statements called the Degree Qualifications Profile (DQP). The DQP defines and measures the general knowledge and skills that students should have obtained upon earning degrees at three degree levels: associate, bachelor's, and master's. The statements are useful as external benchmarks against which institutions can examine the adequacy and coverage of their own learning-outcomes statements. DQP statements also provide guidance about how appropriate outcomes statements should be constructed and illustrate the kinds of student performances that might demonstrate mastery. They are equally useful as a guide for developing new learning outcomes statements. Board members should ask academic leaders if they are aware of the DQP and how it can be used.[8]

---

is especially important for board members to ask the administration to (1) review the established assessment plan well in advance of an accreditation visit, and (2) provide the board with an honest appraisal of overall progress, as well as plans to address any difficulties.

Academic affairs committees, for their part, should understand in more detail how such evidence is collected and used to improve teaching and learning. In reviewing the contents of an assessment plan, committee members need to recognize that there are many appropriate ways to gather evidence about student achievement, and that faculty members are best suited to determine what these might be. Committee members also need to be aware of two important distinctions between different kinds of assessment-based evidence:

First, assessments usually are distinguished as *direct* or *indirect*. Direct assessment methods such as examinations, assignments, and tasks demand that the ability in question be observed palpably and immediately. Indirect assessment, in contrast, uses methods that do not examine learning itself, but rather its consequences—that is, related factors such as job placement, civic participation,

---

[8] Adelman, Cliff; Peter Ewell; Paul Gaston; and Carol Geary Schneider. "The Degree Qualifications Profile." (Lumina Foundation, 2011).

or self-reports about learning gains as provided in questionnaires or interviews. Direct evidence of learning outcomes generally is accorded more credibility than indirect evidence, and all board members should be aware that accreditation now requires at least one form of direct assessment to be used by all institutions for each claimed learning outcome.

Second, assessment can be undertaken using specially designed methods that are applied *outside the normal teaching-learning context*—for example, through the deployment of special examinations, surveys, and behavioral inventories. Alternatively, such evidence can be developed by looking at *existing student work*—including portfolios, work samples, and observations of clinical practice—from a more comprehensive or developmental perspective.

Using naturally occurring examples of student work has the advantage of generating evidence without requiring either special instruments or special attention to ensuring students' motivation to perform. But the abilities that naturally occurring evidence reveals may not completely correspond to the learning outcomes of interest. For example, observation of student performance in a clinical experience in a health-related field may be authentic and unobtrusive, but the clinical encounter itself may not generate an opportunity for the student to reveal an important area of knowledge and skill (such as how to respond to an emergency situation).

As they review assessment results, members of the academic affairs committee should know that there are substantial advantages to using naturally occurring assessment opportunities that are built directly into the curriculum. But they also should be aware that specially constructed examinations or demonstrations administered outside the curriculum and capable of being compared across institutions or programs may be more comprehensive and useful under a different set of circumstances.

The following are among the most common assessment methods used by colleges and universities, together with their most important advantages and challenges:

- **Examinations.** Examinations are the approach most commonly associated with the assessment of student-learning outcomes. Standardized multiple-choice tests are familiar to board members, and their results typically are used to compare institutions or programs. But faculty-constructed examinations, whether administered in class or as capstone demonstrations of mastery at the completion of a program, can be equally valuable as evidence of attainment if they are deliberately constructed around a defined set of learning outcomes.

Evidence based on examinations of either kind is direct and, if collected using standardized examinations, reliably comparable across settings. Accordingly, the evidence tends to be highly credible for external stakeholders. Still, examinations are sometimes limited in their ability to assess mastery or deeper forms of learning, especially if they are confined to multiple-choice formats. Fortunately, exams like the CLA and the CAT, which are not based on multiple-choice formats, allow for a deeper, more rigorous assessment of student learning.

- **Tasks and demonstrations.** Tasks and demonstrations require students to directly apply their knowledge and skills in a particular setting to provide evidence of a desired level of performance. The tasks may be deliberately constructed to generate such evidence (for example, a proof in mathematics or an engineering design), or they may occur naturally in the course of a learning experience (for example, during an internship or clinical encounter). Evidence based on such events is direct, but it also may be difficult to interpret consistently. As a result, effective use of tasks and demonstrations as credible evidence of attainment requires the careful design and deployment of interpretive tools such as scoring guides or rubrics that describe each level of desired performance in some detail.

- **Student work.** This broad category of evidence potentially includes all of the work products generated naturally by students in a particular course of study, including written assignments, examinations, problems, laboratory reports, and field or clinical performances. Although such evidence has the advantage of having already been collected, a great deal of effort is usually involved in meaningfully assembling and interpreting it. As a result, most institutions using this approach sample students' work products, then apply scoring guides or rubrics to draw conclusions about attainment.

Probably the most common method for assembling student work is the *portfolio*, in which selected examples of a given student's work are chosen and examined together. Portfolios may be constructed analytically (for example, by choosing one or two pieces of work deliberately to serve as illustrations of a given outcome), or they may be constructed to reflect development over time by including pieces of work that exemplify the same outcome at different stages of a student's academic career. Finally, scoring criteria can be built directly into the grading process and the results aggregated for later interpretation.

- **Behavioral outcomes.** Student behaviors before and after graduation can provide useful indirect-assessment information. For students in career-preparation programs, for example, job placement and advancement in their field of study commonly is used as a measure of program success, as is participation in graduate study or continuing professional development. Other later behaviors frequently claimed as success measures for both institutions and programs include civic behaviors such as voting and volunteering, lifestyle behaviors such as health and consumption habits, or social and geographic mobility—all of which are related to intended outcomes. In most cases, such evidence is collected by surveys of graduates and former students.

- **Self-reporting.** A final method of obtaining indirect evidence about the attainment of student-learning outcomes is through the testimony of students themselves. Generally, students or graduates are simply asked to rate their own current levels of knowledge or skill across a set of areas that correspond to the learning outcomes in question. Most self-reports are collected by means of questionnaires, but alternative methods include focus groups and telephone or individual interviews.

Institutions tend to rely on evidence based on self-reports because of the ease and efficiency with which such information can be collected, as well as the fact that self-reports are the only method available for obtaining evidence on such non-cognitive outcomes as attitudes, beliefs, and dispositions. Still, debate continues about the validity and reliability of self-reports as proxy measures of actual student attainment. Further, while considerable research has established consistent positive relationships between actual and claimed attainment, self-reports are generally more credible for student behaviors, which are only indirectly related to learning outcomes.

Significantly, few college faculty members are trained during their graduate preparation to design any of these assessment approaches or interpret the resulting data. As a result, members of the academic affairs committee should ask explicitly about their institution's efforts to ensure that faculty members are being supported in their efforts to (1) develop assessable learning-outcomes statements and (2) design effective methods to gather evidence of student achievement. Some support may be provided through a campus institute or a faculty development center; assembling relevant publications on how to construct effective assessments, as well as underwriting faculty attendance at assessment workshops, may also be worthwhile. The form of support is less important than the fact that attention is being paid to the nearly universal need for faculty development in assessment.

3. *Are we benchmarking performance against external standards?*

Many assessment programs now include at least a few sources of evidence that are comparable across institutions or against national norms. Institutions have designed their programs this way for a number of reasons:

First, comparative performance is increasingly being raised as a part of growing demands by states and accrediting organizations for increased accountability. South Dakota currently requires comparative performance on standardized tests for public colleges and universities, just as they do in elementary and secondary schools. Other states are likely to join them. Institutional accrediting organizations also are rapidly moving in the direction of asking institutions how their assessment results compare with some external standard.

At least as important from a board's perspective, external benchmarks of performance on learning outcomes can help an institution determine its areas of comparative advantage against peer institutions or against those with which it competes for students. And in some areas, institutions have used comparative assessment results of several kinds in their student recruitment campaigns.

Members of the academic affairs committee will want to be aware of the kinds of external benchmarks that are available:

- **Standardized national examinations.** A first source of external benchmarks is the array of nationally normed standardized achievement tests. Several testing companies have developed such examinations especially for program and institutional evaluation in higher education. A number of institutions use them periodically to see how their students stack up against national performance levels and to calibrate their own, locally developed assessment approaches. Some of these examinations, such as ACT's Collegiate Assessment of Academic Proficiency (CAAP) and the Educational Testing Service's Measure of Academic Proficiency and Progress (MAPP), assess general skills such as writing, critical thinking, and problem solving. The CLA and CAT, mentioned earlier, are later developments that are not based on a multiple-choice format.

  Other national assessments assess performance in specific fields of study. For example, ETS offers Major Field Achievement Tests in 12 fields, based on their well-known Graduate Record Examinations (GREs). All of these examinations allow institutions to compare the performance of their students against national norms, and many allow comparisons against tailored comparison groups selected by institutions themselves.

  Despite the ready use of examinations in benchmarking, committee members should know that they have many drawbacks. Because their content is determined externally, it may not match the content of the curriculum actually being taught at the institution. And because performance on these examinations does not usually count toward a grade, students may not be even inclined to take them, or to try their best if they do. What's more, faculty may be wary of such examinations because of suspicion that they do not test authentic mastery of student abilities in sufficient depth. Consequently, board members should refrain from advocating specific approaches, though they may be attracted to standardized testing in principle. In their regular reviews of assessment results, members of the academic affairs committee should ask whether any such benchmarking examinations have been considered. If such exams have been considered and rejected, committee members should probe and discuss specific reasons why this is the case.

- **Licensure and certification examinations.** Another source of external benchmarks is the aggregate set of results of the licensure and certification examinations typically taken by students in professional programs. Such exams are especially common in the health professions, but also show up in such fields as accounting, engineering, and teacher education. States frequently compile pass rates on the exams, and institutions may use those rates as institutional-performance measures and as comparisons with national or state norms and with the results of other institutions. Members of the academic affairs committee should monitor which examinations are taken by the institution's graduates and how the graduates perform. But they should be aware that performance on such examinations—as on virtually all examinations—depends a lot on student background and academic aptitude. As a result, they should ask academic administrators how best to interpret and use the results.

- **Consortia.** Additionally, some institutions have formed data-sharing consortia to obtain external benchmarks for their assessments. Such consortia are voluntary groups of reasonably similar institutions that arrange to share results on common assessments—generally on a confidential basis—to assist them in their own program-improvement efforts. Most of the groups use the kinds of common examinations already described, but some have developed their own. Institutional consortia also can be helpful in aligning locally designed assessments by arranging for faculty at different institutions to review one another's assessment methods, scoring rubrics, and standards. Some institutions have even provided one another's programs with "external examiners" to look at student performance on a selected basis to see whether academic standards are comparable across institutions.

Committee members should recognize that forming such partnerships is a significant investment. But if no other appropriate ways are available to establish external points of comparison for the institution's assessment efforts, board members should nonetheless ask whether academic leaders and faculty have considered this route.

Finally, board and committee members should remember that not everything can or should be benchmarked to an external standard. Establishing valid external points of comparison is always tricky, and the process should not be approached mechanically or universally. It is completely appropriate that most assessment methods be developed locally and not be tied to any such standard. If the primary goal of assessment is program improvement, it is far more important that the assessments being used fit the program's goals and context than whether they are externally benchmarked. But it certainly is important for the board to periodically ask the more general question of how the administration assures itself that the assessment results it obtains are adequate and appropriate.

4. *Who is responsible for assessment, and how is it accomplished?*

Institutional assessment programs should have a clear organizational structure on campus, with appropriate lines of responsibility and accountability. Because the board is responsible for guaranteeing that the right management structures are in place for ensuring academic quality, it is part of its business to know what those structures look like. Just as important, the fact that the institution has a visible structure for assessment—something that can actually be looked at during a campus visit—is an important part of accreditation reviews. Once again, the academic affairs committee typically will be familiar with the organizational structure, and its members should periodically ask academic leaders whether it is appropriately resourced and functioning properly.

That said, there is no single approach to organizing assessment that fits the needs and contexts of all colleges and universities. Virtually all have an assessment committee charged with general oversight of the assessment function. Sometimes this committee is a formal part of the faculty governance structure—usually as a subcommittee of the academic planning or strategic planning committee— but sometimes it is part of the administrative committee structure that is advisory to the chief academic officer.

> " No single approach to organizing assessment fits the needs and contexts of all colleges and universities. "

Either choice is reasonable, depending upon the institution's circumstances. But because assessment is fundamentally a faculty responsibility, the membership and organization of the committee should clearly signal that the faculty has the leading role in developing the assessment process and seeing that it is carried out properly. Board members should know the reasons why oversight of the assessment function is organized the way it is, and should be assured that such a governance structure includes significant faculty involvement and is not simply run by the administration.

Growing numbers of colleges and universities are also establishing assessment offices under the direction of an assessment coordinator to assist the faculty in designing and administering assessments. Generally, the offices are staffed by one or more individuals who have a background in testing and measurement, psychology, or the social sciences and who are drawn from either outside the institution or from its own faculty. At some institutions, the assessment coordinator is housed in and coordinated by a faculty-development or teaching and learning center; at others, dedicated assessment staffing is added to the office of institutional research. Again, there is no right answer to the question of how best to create an organizational support structure for the necessarily decentralized process of assessment, which relies on the efforts of individual academic departments to do most of the work. But board members, and particularly members of the academic affairs committee, should know what resources are in place, who is responsible for them, and the reasons for these particular arrangements.

5. *How do we use assessment results?*

A recent national survey of chief academic officers conducted by the National Institute for Learning Outcomes Assessment (NILOA) found that one of the biggest challenges institutions face with regard to assessment is using the evidence the process generates to improve teaching and learning.[9] That may come as a surprise to board members since continuous improvement is supposed to be a principal reason for doing assessment in the first place. But all too often, institutions become engaged in assessment due primarily to external requirements—then, in the press of implementation, fail to systematically "close the loop" by carefully considering the implications of what they find and acting accordingly. Allowing that to happen is a mistake. Accreditors are not looking for a set of assessment procedures so much as they are seeking an institutional culture of evidence-based management that emphasizes action as well as data collection. And even if external accountability requirements were not present, running an expensive assessment process without using the results it generates is simply a waste of resources. For both of those reasons, board members should keep an eye on how assessment results are used.

In asking academic administrators how and where they use assessment results, board members should know that there are a number of places where they might expect to see the results applied:

- **As part of the performance indicator system that many institutions have established to monitor their condition and effectiveness.** Some colleges and universities include such measures as performance on externally benchmarked examinations, selected alumni survey results, or in-field job-placement rates on the "dashboards" they have created to track their performance. This is one of the most important connections for boards to ask about because such dashboards are intended to provide guidance about

---

[9] Kuh, George and Stanley Ikenberry. "More Than You Think, Less Than We Need: Learning Outcomes Assessment in American Higher Education." Urbana, IL: University of Illinois and Indiana University, National Institute for Learning Outcomes Assessment (NILOA), 2009.

strategic direction and to track progress on established institutional priorities—priorities that the board at minimum has reviewed and approved or, preferably, helped establish in the first place.

- **In program or departmental reviews.** Many institutions have established cyclical processes in which each academic program or department is examined every five to seven years—a process that usually involves a brief self-study and a systematic examination by an internal review panel. (*See Chapter 5.*) Increasingly, institutions are including an explicit assessment component in their program-review processes because the familiar framework of program review provides a ready-made opportunity to assemble and consider program-level assessment results.

  Some institutions, however, do not have an established program-review process around which to organize the assessment process. Most that do not instead use a specially devised program-level assessment reporting mechanism through which each department presents an annual or biennial description of how it gathers assessment evidence, what it has found in the latest cycle, and how the results have been used. Regardless, academic affairs committees provide a natural venue for examining program-level assessment results and discussing their implications with academic and faculty leaders. Members of the committee should ask specifically about how these program-level reports are used, just as they should ask about how the results of surveys or of general education assessments have been used. Committee members should be especially interested in how such information can help inform strategic decisions. They might ask, for example, which of the programs provide good opportunities for expansion, or which programs that are especially important to the institution's mission are underperforming and therefore need attention and investment.

- **In the budgeting process.** Although most internal budgetary decisions are driven by established expenditure commitments, every institution engages in some form of strategic budgeting through which additional resources are allocated to support new strategic initiatives and needs. In their involvement with strategic planning, boards are involved in setting and approving the priorities used to guide such expenditures, and rely on institutional leaders to provide the specific evidence of effectiveness to help identify those priorities. Academic affairs committees, in turn, may be more directly involved in setting strategic investment priorities for academic programs, for improving instruction, or for faculty development. Assessment evidence can prove especially important in these deliberations because it can clearly identify programmatic or instructional strengths on which to build or shortcomings in teaching and learning that need attention.

- **In student recruitment.** Assessment results have been heavily used as a marketing tool by for-profit institutions in the realm of job placement and licensure passage. Board members should ask what assessment results reveal about particular areas of success for graduates and how that information might help the institution's efforts to better position itself in an increasingly competitive market.

Whatever the application, boards should ensure that assessment results are used *strategically*—that is, to help identify opportunities for investment that will further leverage institutional mission. And finally, boards should ask that the assessment process is itself periodically assessed to see whether it is organized appropriately, whether its methods of gathering evidence of student achievement are sound and appropriate, and whether its results are usable and being used. Although assessment programs are relatively new at most campuses, it is easy for those responsible for them to fall into a routine and become complacent. Every institution should take a periodic, systematic look at its entire assessment operation—perhaps once every five years—to ensure that it is working as planned and to suggest enhancements or deletions. In this regard, academic affairs committees might make it a particular point to ask academic leaders each year about what is working well in assessment, what challenges have been encountered, and what could be improved.

RETENTION, GRADUATION, AND STUDENT "FLOW"

In an era of constrained financial resources, maintaining enrollment is of paramount importance to colleges and universities. Equally pressing are (1) institutions' need to raise the success rates of their students (that is, the number of students who persist to graduation) from varying backgrounds to achieve publicly stated goals about raising national degree-attainment levels; and (2) public concerns about the "educational pipeline." In response, institutions are devoting greater attention to monitoring and shaping the characteristics of their undergraduate student bodies. Recruitment programs are being more carefully targeted to boost the probability that a given student will complete the program, and retention programs are being developed with much greater sensitivity to the need for different kinds of advising and intervention strategies for different kinds of students.

Nevertheless, an average of only 59 percent of entering four-year college freshmen complete their programs within six years at the institution in which they started, and 30 percent of entering two-year college students do so within three years, according to the National Center for Education Statistics.[10] Board members need to understand, however, that such statistics do not tell the whole story about the complex phenomenon of student flow through the nation's higher education system.

---

[10] National Center for Education Statistics, "Graduation rates of first-time postsecondary students, 1996 through 2007," U.S. Department of Education (2011); http://nces.ed.gov/programs/digest/d11/tables/ dt11_345.asp

■ THE BASICS

The Limitations of Graduation-Rate Data

Graduation-rate statistics (such as those compiled by the NCES) are limited to students who enroll full time and are attending college for the first time. Given the high levels of part-time enrollments and new transfers typical at many institutions, such statistics may be only partially representative. At some community colleges, for example, full-time, first-time students may constitute fewer than 10 percent of any entering group. Furthermore, such statistics don't account for the growing trend of students attending multiple institutions in pursuit of a degree—yet according to a U.S. Department of Education study, more than two-thirds of students who ultimately earn a bachelor's degree attended two or more institutions to do so (and more than a fifth attended three or more).[11] On the one hand, this growing "enrollment swirl" tends to depress the graduation rates of individual institutions. But on the other hand, more-frequent transfer tends to increase the overall rate of baccalaureate attainment. Some studies, for example, suggest that almost 70 percent of those who enter college will have earned a bachelor's degree somewhere by the time they are 25.[12]

Such figures reflect the difficulty of determining patterns of student flow at the institutional level—yet doing so is a crucial part of academic-quality management. In addition to the financial implications of student dropouts, student success is an important indicator of the overall quality of an academic program. If academically qualified students are leaving in large numbers, there is surely a problem present that ought to be looked at even though the remaining graduates perform well.

Despite their limitations, graduation-rate statistics nonetheless define the reputations of all but the most selective institutions—and they have become the

---

[11] Adelman, Clifford. *Answers in the Toolbox: Academic Intensity, Attendance Patterns, and Bachelor's Degree Attainment.* Washington, DC: Office of Vocational and Continuing Education, U.S. Department of Education (1999).

[12] Adelman, Clifford. *The Toolbox Revisited: Paths to Degree Completion from High School Through College.* Washington, DC: Office of Vocational and Continuing Education, U.S. Department of Education (2006).

most commonly used measures of institutional performance in higher education. Virtually all states require public institutions to report their graduation rates, while the federal Student Right-to-Know and Campus Security Act requires *all* institutions eligible for federal financial-aid funding to disclose their graduation rates to prospective students and their parents. Furthermore, the importance of examining graduation rates, as well as the factors underlying them, have become prominent topics in institutional accreditation reviews. Consequently, boards need to know how their institutions are performing on such measures. Boards must also ensure that academic administrators have the information they need about institutional student flow so that they can intervene to increase student success rates.

Understanding Retention and Graduation Statistics

All colleges and universities are required by law to report to the federal government their three-year or six-year graduation rates for full-time, first-time students, compiled according to a standard methodology and broken down by gender and by race/ethnicity. To comply, institutions—usually through the registrar or office of institutional research—calculate retention and graduation statistics from information maintained in institutional student-registration systems. All such statistics are calculated on a so-called "cohort" basis, which means that a group of entering students are selected at a particular point in time (in the case of federal reporting, students who entered the institution for the first time in the fall term), then tracked to a point in time six years later (or three, in the case of community colleges) to determine how many have earned their degrees.

The basic graduation rate is then calculated by dividing those members of the original group who have completed their degrees within the designated period by the total number who originally started. Retention-rate calculations are similar and generally are calculated for first-year students returning for a second year. (NCES is currently in the process of revising its methods for calculating graduation rates to take part-time students and incoming transfers into account, but those changes will not be in place for a number of years.)

When interpreting the retention and graduation statistics provided by institutional leaders, board members should know what factors generally influence the numbers. The most important drivers of overall retention and graduation are *institutional selectivity* and *student academic ability*. All other things equal, highly selective institutions significantly outperform institutions with open admissions in overall graduation rates. And all institutions are more likely to retain students with higher SAT or ACT scores than students with lower scores. Additionally, independent institutions generally have higher retention and graduation rates than public institutions. Other factors that tend to be positively related to higher retention and graduation rates include full-time continuous attendance, direct entry out of high school, and sufficient financial-aid support. Factors that tend to be negatively related to higher rates are nontraditional student characteristics (older, part-time), minority status (especially black and Hispanic), lower household income, and first-generation college attendance.

It is important to emphasize, however, that these factors are not always definitive in matters of retention and graduation: Many institutions of modest selectivity retain students at higher rates than their peers, while others fail to retain their brightest students. Institutional commitments and actions matter a lot in the area of student success. *All* institutions can improve their performance.

A Call for Strong Leadership

Heightened board attention to issues of academic quality and graduation and retention can be particularly helpful in encouraging institutional leaders to pay close attention to those issues. Strong institutional leadership is essential, as demonstrated by recent research that emphasizes graduation rates.[13] That research shows that exemplary institutions not only have the proper programs and resources in place, but also are led by presidents who call atten-

---

[13] See Kuh, George D.; Kinzie, Jillian; Schuh, John H.; Whitt, Elizabeth J.; and Associates. *Student Success in College.* (Jossey-Bass, 2005). See also: American Association of State Colleges and Universities, "The Graduation Rate Outcomes Project" (AASCU, 2005).

tion to the institution's commitment to student success. Partly thanks to such vigorous and visible presidential leadership, faculty and staff at exemplary colleges display a proactive readiness to help students who are struggling. Finally, institutions that are the most successful at student retention take evidence seriously: They have developed sophisticated ways of analyzing available data about student flow that lets them understand how particular kinds of students are experiencing the institution, what can be done to improve these experiences, and how to monitor the progress and effectiveness of efforts to improve student success. As in all other areas of academic-quality assurance, boards should make sure such data resources are in place and are being used.

> **" Exemplary colleges display a proactive readiness to help students who are struggling. "**

QUESTIONS FOR BOARDS TO CONSIDER

Because understanding the nuances of statistics about student success is a challenge, board members should be careful not to over-interpret such measures. Understanding what goes into graduation rates and what these statistics really mean is important, however. Meanwhile, managing student flow to create the right kinds of efficiencies and to intervene effectively to maximize student success is a job that faculty and staff need to be doing every day—and presidents need to motivate them to continue. Once boards are assured that those things are being done, they need to ask for periodic reports on effectiveness and then stay out of the way.

Following are the key big-picture questions that board members ought to ask when they request periodic status reports:

1. *What are our basic indicators of student progression and success?*
All institutions must provide the federal government with such statistics and make them available to prospective students and their parents through the institutions' Web sites, catalogues, or recruiting publications. But those requirements

don't necessarily mean that leaders are really studying the numbers, determining what they mean, and tailoring active and continuous steps to improve performance. Instead, at many institutions, such reporting is simply a routine operational task that goes no farther. That is not acceptable.

Boards need to ensure that institutional leaders are monitoring and utilizing retention and graduation data. Boards can prevent complacency in the administration by asking that results of the federal Graduation Rate Survey (GRS) be reported to them each year, along with more-conventional statistics such as admissions and enrollment numbers. Boards should also know how and in what format the required statistics are disclosed to stakeholders, and should ask administrators to discuss with them the institution's results and the implications.

In asking such questions, boards are signaling the importance they attach to the institution's efforts to improve student success. But they probably will discover that there are more-effective ways to measure the institution's success than the federally mandated statistics. As discussed earlier, the required measures may leave out substantial proportions of the institution's entering students. Moreover, results for community-college transfer students (and the institutions they attend) may be especially skewed, as many students are successful precisely because they transfer to four-year institutions to finish earning their degrees. As a result, boards should ask administrators what indicators *they* use in monitoring overall student success and in managing their efforts to improve it. If the administration's measures are different from those that are publicly reported, boards need to know the reasons why and what additional insights those measures provide.

Many such discussions are likely to be the purview of the academic affairs committee, since measures of student flow bear on the curriculum and patterns of student course-taking and other academic behavior. But because retention is also an aspect of enrollment management, related discussions are likely among board committees that deal with competitiveness, marketing, and student affairs as well. Just as it is difficult to assign issues concerning student progress to any one administrative office, it also is tough to limit those discussions to any given board committee. As a result, the board as a whole should ensure that the president and senior administrators are paying attention.

Finally, on whatever basis the administration determines how well the institution is performing with respect to retention and program completion, boards ought to ask for an estimate of the cost of attrition. All enrolled students reflect the institutional costs associated with recruiting them and ensuring that they will matriculate. If a given student leaves, another will need to be recruited to take his or her place. Every student who leaves represents lost tuition revenue (and for some institutions, state subsidies as well). Although it is conventional wisdom that it is easier to retain a current student than to recruit a new one, that may not be true at all institutions; in many cases, these costs cannot be calculated precisely. Presidents ought to be able to discuss with the board the broad financial consequences for the institution associated with students who fail to complete their programs.

2. *How does our performance measure up?*

Boards need to know something about the institution's comparative performance on retention and graduation measures. That means using publicly reported statistics obtained from the Graduation Rate Survey or, for public institutions, from comparative institutional statistics reported by the system office or state higher education coordinating board. As noted earlier, comparing institutional outcomes on these measures is tricky: Performance will vary naturally based on institutional characteristics such as selectivity and program offerings as well as on student characteristics. Comparisons with national averages are, consequently, not very helpful, making it far better to compare the institution's outcomes with those of institutions sharing similar characteristics.

> **"Compare the institution's outcomes with those of institutions sharing similar characteristics."**

One useful vehicle for making such comparisons is an online tool called College Results Online, available from the Washington-based Education Trust at www.collegeresults.org. After a user enters the name of an institution, the system selects a set of peer institutions based on such characteristics as size, admissions-test scores, minority and part-time enrollment, financial-aid need, and academic-program offerings. The site then displays comparison charts that show how the selected institution stacks up against its peers with respect to graduation and other characteristics. The site also may be used to compare a set of user-selected peer institutions directly, which may be useful if the institution has an established group of institutions against which it regularly compares performance. Consulting College Results Online may be useful for board members, if only to make them aware of the considerable variation in retention and graduation rates across different kinds of colleges and universities.

Another source of such comparisons are the various voluntary accountability reporting templates that have recently been developed by higher education associations.[14] These templates include reporting on degree completion and retention using standard formats and, because they are made public, are accessible for peer institutions. Board committees concerned with marketing or admissions may find this comparative information especially useful in discussions with institutional leaders—especially when discussing an institution's relative performance against its competitors.

For public institutions, other sources of comparative information include reports posted annually by state system or coordinating boards. Boards should (1) ensure that administrators are aware of these additional resources and (2) ask the administration to explain any differences in performance between the institution and its peers and any implications such differences might have for action.

3. *What does success look like for different kinds of students?*

Overall retention and graduation rates tell only a limited story about student success at any institution. Regardless of its general enrollment profile, every institution has different subgroups of students defined by different combinations of

---

[14] For example, the Voluntary System of Accountability (VSA) designed by the American Association of Public Land Grant Universities (APLU) and the American Association of State Colleges and Universities (AASCU); the Voluntary Framework of Accountability (VFA) designed by the American Association of Community Colleges (AACC); and Transparency by Design (TbD) designed by the Western Cooperative for Educational Technology (WCET).

characteristics. While the details differ from institution to institution, typical subpopulations include student athletes, adult or part-time students, students who live in residence halls, commuter students, minority students, students with known academic challenges, and students who receive financial aid. (The board may be especially interested in the latter group, and especially in those students receiving *institutional* aid, because the board will want to be certain the institution is investing its own money as fully as possible in those most likely to succeed.)

Each subpopulation may experience a different pattern of success as it moves through the institution. An overall graduation rate is simply the combination of these diverse subpopulation rates, which may differ from one another. In fact, institutions are frequently fooled into believing they have improved retention rates through improved programming when all they have really done is changed the enrollment proportions among various subpopulations that have different retention rates.

Consequently, board members need to ask: How are different kinds of students faring in terms of retention and graduation? Federal reporting already requires institutions to break down retention and graduation rates by gender and race/ethnicity, so those rates should be readily available. But in addition, boards should ask:

- Which types of students are experiencing the highest success rates, and which the lowest?
- How much of a difference exists between the least and most successful groups, and is it significant or substantive enough to worry about?
- What have been the trends over time with respect to different subgroups' performances?

In asking those questions, it is important to explore the administration's own views of which subgroups it thinks are most important to the institution's success and how their experiences are likely to differ. But board members should first be aware of the fact that effective intervention strategies usually differ for different kinds of students. Successful institutions do not embark on generic, one-size-fits-all retention efforts that treat everybody the same; instead, those institutions recognize that student success requires careful coordination of a range of strategies targeted at different student populations—each of which has a particular set of retention challenges. (The concept is similar to the notion of "market segmentation," with which some board members already may be familiar through discussions about student recruitment.) The board needs to determine that academic and student affairs leaders are thinking about subpopulations and their relative differences and are examining approaches that take those differences into account.

That said, there are a number of important distinctions to keep in mind when disaggregating graduation and retention rates:

- First, it is useful to know whether students who left the institution did so for *academic* or *nonacademic* reasons. A usual breakdown is whether a given student was in good academic standing during his or her last term of enrollment; overall grade-point averages also are frequently used to make this distinction. So while it is understandable that some students having academic difficulty may drop out, every student who leaves for nonacademic reasons represents a case that may have been preventable and raises questions about what might be done in the future to prevent such losses.

- Second, it is useful to know not only *which kinds* of students dropped out but also *when* they did so. National statistics, as well as substantial research at the campus level, suggest that most students are at risk in their first year—frequently making the provisional decision to leave early in their first term, though they may not act on it right away. Their reasons often include early bad experiences with services provided, perceived lack of fit with the institution and its culture, an inability to connect socially with anyone at the institution, and so forth.

On the other hand, students in good academic standing who withdraw later—say, in the second or third year—are much more likely to leave for programmatic reasons. Those reasons might include an inability to find the right major (but finding it available at a different institution) or a decision to switch programs or potential careers.

Boards should ensure that administrators have made these basic distinctions in the way they are looking at retention data and are following up on the implied programmatic remedies.

4. *Who is accountable for student success, and what are we doing to improve our performance?*

Student success is everybody's job, but often nobody's explicit responsibility. The result is that many institutions lack a coherent program aimed at increasing success, and instead rely on well-intentioned but unfocused efforts from various members of the academic and administrative staffs. It is the job of institutional leaders to organize those disparate efforts.

For example, the student affairs staff is on the front lines of the effort, providing counseling, programming, financial aid, and a range of other services. But those services are too frequently provided piecemeal and with little guidance regarding an overarching goal.

Faculty members, too, are critical to the effort to foster student success, particularly since students' academic-advisement and classroom experiences crucially shape their impressions and attitudes during their first year of attendance. Isolated in individual classrooms, however, some faculty members deal only with limited aspects of their students' academic careers (unless they also act as those students' advisers). More important, some faculty members do not see student retention as part of their jobs because they are focused strictly on teaching and research in their individual disciplines.

Athletics directors are also deeply concerned about retention and success for student athletes. The National Collegiate Athletic Association directly monitors graduation rates for student athletes, and institutions can lose eligibility if performance is too low. Some collegiate athletics departments have developed their own exemplary academic and counseling/support programs that other parties on campus may learn from.

Finally, every other employee at the institution—groundskeepers, maintenance workers, food-service employees, bursar's clerks, campus security—can play a role in student satisfaction and success. Any of them may touch, or fail to touch, students in a meaningful way. Any of them may affect a particular student's success. But first, they have to know how to behave appropriately in their roles, and somebody must be responsible for seeing that they do.

Given the potential contributions of so many campus employees, presidents play a crucial role in focusing those efforts and building a campus oriented toward student success. Consequently, boards need to ensure that active efforts to retain and graduate students are near the top of the president's agenda. But they also need to know the president's thinking about how the institution is *organized* to carry out this vital task.

> **❝A prevailing faculty and staff attitude must be to help *all* students achieve their potential.❞**

At some institutions, organizational responsibility for student success belongs to a particular office or individual. At others, it is assumed to be part of the mission of every academic department and support unit, with contributions to retention and student-success programming made a visible part of the accountability review for chairs and directors, and actively overseen by the appropriate vice presidents. There is no one "right" recipe for how to organize student-success efforts, and much depends on history, campus culture, and presidential leadership style. But board members need to know how it is done on their campus, why, and whether or not it is working. At the same time, boards should be broadly familiar with the kinds of student-success programs that have proved effective across multiple settings. (*See "What Works In Student-Success Programming," page 57.*)

Numerous reviews have cited practices that include "learning communities," and early skills-assessment and remediation as being effective in increasing student success; boards should be aware of those practices. But it is important to stress that those reviews also emphasize that "sound programming" alone is not sufficient to guarantee success. Rather, strong programming must instead be developed and delivered in the nexus of a campus culture that emphasizes high expectations for students, a belief that any student admitted can succeed in meeting these expectations, and a prevailing attitude among faculty and staff that helping all students to achieve their potential is an integral part of their everyday work.

Building a culture of student success is of strategic importance both because of the negative fiscal impact of low graduation rates and because poor performance shapes public and marketplace perceptions of the institution's quality.

What Works In Student-Success Programming

Some of the most prominent and proven efforts include the following:

- **First-year experience programs** that begin with new-student orientation and continue throughout a student's first term or year, involving special programming to help students acclimate to college, learn to use academic resources such as the library, develop good study and work habits, and foster engagement through strong peer relationships;

- **Early assessment of student's basic skills**, followed by effective mandatory placement and remediation if deficiencies are detected;

- **Academic "early warning" systems** that provide faculty with a channel to quickly telegraph student difficulties to advisement or student affairs staff who can promptly intervene to provide the necessary help;

- **Proactive student-advisement arrangements** that help students internalize what is expected of them and that provide them with clear "pathways" through the curriculum that are effective for learning and that students understand;

- **Flexible and understandable procedures** for providing necessary services such as financial aid and registration;

- **Integrated student-service centers** that provide "one-stop shopping" for such services as advising, counseling, financial aid, registration, tutoring, academic support, and health care; and

- **Specific curricular features such as "learning communities"** that involve groups of students taking common content-linked coursework their first year, internships and other service-learning opportunities, and student research programs that promote frequent and meaningful contact between faculty and students.

Active presidential commitment and leadership are crucial for fostering such a culture. Active board interest in the reality behind graduation and retention statistics may help busy presidents keep student success near the top of their agendas.

LISTENING TO STAKEHOLDERS AND "CUSTOMERS"

It should seem logical to most board members that colleges and universities periodically survey their students and alumni. After all, seeking customer feedback is a practice of every sound business. But the results of such evidence gathering, done right, also can provide an important source of information for academic-quality assurance and improvement.

Using the term "customers" in connection with students will not always be welcome among academics. After all, use of this term conjures up all kinds of unsavory images like students "buying" grades, or even credentials. Yet in some important ways, students are very much consumers of their higher education experiences, and it is appropriate to consider them as such. For example, most students choose which college to attend, and their satisfaction once enrolled, as expressed to family and friends, may be decisive in influencing their peers to make the same choice. Students are direct consumers of their colleges' academic offerings, campus facilities, and services, and they are the best experts on their satisfaction with those experiences. And, of course, students participate in a range of processes run by the institution, such as registration and financial aid.

Still, academics have a point when they argue that viewing students only as customers may be a wrong-headed way to look at the teaching and learning process. If pressed to use a corporate or manufacturing analogy, faculty members are more likely to consider students unfinished "raw materials" that are transformed by what the institution does to yield a "value-added" product. Further stretching the analogy in a way more amenable to the views of educators, students also are "co-producers" and "managers" of their own learning. *They* are the ones that make important decisions about how much time to spend on various kinds of learning activities and how they actually will use the learning resources the institution puts at their disposal.

Knowing how students make those learning choices and use the resources available to them—as well as understanding the kinds of experiences students seek—are crucial steps in helping academic leaders, faculty members, and staff members understand what is really happening in the teaching and learning process. Consequently, members of the board's academic affairs committee will want to understand students' perspective on their choices as well as the faculty's. To help them do that, committee members should know how to properly review evidence drawn from student surveys, which is essential in determining student motivations and experiences.

■ THE BASICS

National Student Surveys

Although many surveys are typically administered to students by specific campus offices and services, most institutions also regularly conduct a few central survey efforts aimed at current students or alumni. These broader efforts are generally led by the student affairs office or, if the institution has one, the office of institutional research.

Most institutions develop their own surveys, but more and more are also participating in one or more national surveys to enable comparative benchmarking. Among the most prominent are the following:

- **The CIRP Freshman Survey**. The CIRP Freshman Survey—offered by the Cooperative Institutional Research Program, based out of UCLA's Higher Education Research Institute—is the longest-running student survey effort in higher education. The survey generally makes national news each year when it releases its findings about the attitudes and characteristics of the nation's entering freshman classes. The survey is comprehensive, and includes questions about topics ranging from students' values, political views, and family backgrounds to their academic experiences in high school and perceived preparation levels. (CIRP also conducts a follow-up survey containing parallel items for graduates a decade after their freshman year.)

- **The National Survey of Student Engagement (NSSE)**. Conducted by Indiana University's Center for Postsecondary Research, the NSSE (commonly referred to as "Nessie") explicitly examines experiences and curricular features that prior research has demonstrated to be associated with substantive gains in learning—including such factors as frequent and meaningful student-faculty contact, time spent studying and in other academic pursuits, active and experience-based learning opportunities, and a supportive campus environment. The survey is administered simultaneously to sample groups of freshmen who are at the end of their first year and seniors who are about to graduate. A parallel survey effort for two-year colleges is the **Community College Survey of Student Engagement (CCSSE)**, administered by the Center for Community College Student Engagement at the University of Texas, Austin.

  > **If an institution has never used one of these surveys for benchmarking, ask why.**

- **The College Student Experience Questionnaire (CSEQ)**. The CSEQ (also conducted by Indiana University University's Center for Postsecondary Research) provides a more in-depth look at students' academic experiences by looking explicitly at the use of various academic resources provided by their institutions. This includes students' use of the library, their participation in different kinds of courses and out-of-class learning experiences, and their academic interaction with their professors and peers. The survey is founded on the notion of "quality of effort"—that is, the level and type of investment that students exhibit in their academic work.

- **The Student Satisfaction Inventory (SSI)**. Offered by Noel-Levitz, Inc., an independent consulting firm specializing in retention work, the SSI comprises a series of surveys that ask students to evaluate the services they receive in terms of their importance to them and how well they believe they are being served. The resulting "performance gap" between importance and satisfaction ratings is the primary analytical tool used in interpreting results.

- **Evaluation Survey Services (ESS).** Offered by ACT, this long-standing family of surveys addresses students' general college experiences, their satisfaction with services and academic offerings, and their self-assessments on a range of student outcomes. Different editions of the survey are tailored to accommodate entering students, continuing students, graduating seniors, and recent alumni.

What Boards Need to Know About
Survey Implementation and Results

All of these national surveys can be administered on a consortium basis with other institutions, and all provide flexible reports involving peer comparisons. All of them also allow institutions to add questions of their own design, which are scored along with the regular items. These advantages are substantial, so if an institution has never used one of them for benchmarking, board members should ask why. There are legitimate reasons for not doing so—including costs and inappropriate survey content in the context of the institution's mission—but raising the question makes this important choice explicit.

Board and committee members should also be generally aware of how and to whom surveys are typically administered, and how the results are interpreted:

- **Administration.** While most surveys used to be administered in class or via mail, the Web is now the most popular medium both because it is inexpensive and because responses arrive already in electronic form.

- **Samples.** To further cut costs, many survey managers administer surveys to only a sample of the target student population instead of to all students. Like public-opinion polling, sampling can yield an accurate pattern of overall response at a fairly low cost. However, the results are accurate only within a specified margin of error (usually about 3 percent to 5 percent), and the smaller the sample, the more difficult it becomes to break down accurately the responses of increasingly smaller subgroups.

- **Interpretation.** Interpreting survey results is mostly about internal comparisons, trends in results over time, and benchmarked comparisons with other institutions. This is because the overall response to a particular survey item may have as much to do with how the question is worded than any underlying condition. Interpreting survey results, then, is generally about looking for patterns of high and low scores across different survey questions or across different surveyed populations. Finally, much less frequently, surveys are supplemented by qualitative study methods such as focus groups and interviews. These usually are accomplished in conjunction with surveys to probe student opinion more deeply.

QUESTIONS FOR BOARDS TO CONSIDER

As in other areas, the board's first concern in the realm of "customer feedback" is to ensure that the institution has such mechanisms in place. The board's second concern should be determining whether or not the overall response pattern indicates widespread satisfaction among students and stakeholders. Finally, if problems are apparent, the board needs to ensure that the administration has a reasonable plan to address them. Beyond questions about those basic fiduciary matters, board members (and especially those on the academic affairs committee) might also appropriately ask the following:

1. *What do students' responses tell us about the quality of their academic experiences?*

As "customers," students naturally will have a lot to report about their satisfaction with direct services, and board members should be sure that the administration is listening. But at a deeper level, boards should inquire about the extent to which student surveys are directed at the essential question of academic quality. This may be a particularly appropriate topic for the academic affairs committee to take up, discuss with academic leaders, and report on to the full board.

First, boards should know what kinds of questions are asked on their institutions' surveys. Surveys such as NSSE, CCSSE, and CSEQ are explicitly designed to solicit students' testimony about the quality of their academic experiences. If institutions use their own surveys, it is appropriate for boards to ask academic administrators about the extent to which they solicit feedback on such matters as experiences with faculty, students' engagement with academic work, and the extent to which they encounter good practices in teaching and learning (such as collaborative work, active and "hands-on" learning experiences, and service or community-based learning).

> **Survey results are more powerful when they can be linked to other kinds of information about student learning experiences.**

Moreover, boards should remember that, as with the results of learning assessments and graduation rates, student testimony about academic quality will differ from one student subpopulation to another. It is therefore useful for committee members to learn not only about the overall response patterns but also about any major differences in perceptions or experiences evident among different kinds of students. Overall averages can be deceptive: For example, survey results may tell us that the average student spends 12.5 hours outside of class per week on academic activities, such as doing assigned reading, writing papers, completing problem sets, or using the library. But within that average, there may be a considerable range of behavior. How many students are spending only an hour or two on these activities, or no time at all? And if substantial numbers of under-engaged students are out there, what are their characteristics?

While the academic affairs committee may look at such results and engage academic leaders in active dialogue about what they should do when survey results suggest lack of engagement, the full board needs to be assured that administrators are probing below the surface to determine whether different patterns of student experience are present.

Student survey results are also much more powerful when they can be linked to other kinds of information about student learning experiences. For example, most student surveys allow institutions the option of assigning student ID numbers or other unique identifiers to survey-takers that will then allow institutions to link to other sources of information about those students. So, for example, by being able to cross-reference a student's transcript, the institution can consider the student's testimony about the quality of her experiences together with what classes she took, in what order she took them, when she declared a major, and similar behavioral information. Likewise, by looking at the student's responses to past or future surveys, the institution can also see how her experience has changed over time. Using all three data points can generate powerful analyses of how students are moving through the institution's curriculum and what is happening to them at each stage. Again, this is a good topic to be raised and discussed periodically by the academic affairs committee.

Similarly, student testimony can be considered together with parallel information drawn from the faculty or student affairs staff. The NSSE program, for instance, sponsors an additional survey, the Faculty Survey of Student Engagement (FSSE), which typically is completed by faculty at the same time students complete NSSE. Comparing results from the two surveys allows for an exploration of the contrasts and areas of agreement between student and faculty perceptions of the learning experience. Many institutions that have used this approach have found that the faculty's expectations of student time on task or levels of class preparation to be far in excess of what students actually say they are doing—a contrast that has provoked a good deal of discussion and reaction. A similar approach could be used with any of the student surveys an institution might use.

Above all, board members should recognize that survey results aren't just valuable as data points. The results are also essential starting points for discussions among academic leaders, faculty, and administrators about how learning is occurring, what may be hindering it, and how the institution is using survey opportunities to stimulate reflective conversations about teaching and learning.

2. *How confident can we be about what we've found?*

On the face of it, students' testimony about their experiences seems compelling. After all, students are sharing their own experiences, so their reports should be credible. But in fact, the information that can be drawn from surveys is in some ways limited. If the academic affairs committee begins to delve deeply into student survey results in dialogue with academic and student affairs leaders, its members should be wary of jumping to conclusions about what student responses to survey questions really mean. Boards should pay attention to the following issues:

- **Sample size**. As noted earlier, most surveys are based on samples of students or alumni rather than the entire population. This means that they have a given margin of error at a given level of confidence, both of which depend upon the size of the sample. So a particular survey result—say, 62 percent responding that they are "satisfied" or "very satisfied" with the advising they have received—will really mean something like: "We can be certain that 95 percent of the time between 57 percent and 67 percent of students feel this way."

- **Response rate**. It is fairly certain that not all students who are asked to respond to a given survey actually do so—and the smaller the number of respondents, the greater the need for caution in evaluating the responses. Although some institutions are able to obtain response rates of 75 percent or more to student or alumni surveys, the vast majority of institutions do nowhere near that well. The national response rate for the NSSE survey, which is administered using some of the most sophisticated survey techniques currently available, is 33 percent (down from 42 percent a dozen years ago), and overall student survey response rates have been declining over the past decade. A low response rate does not necessarily compromise results, but it does introduce additional uncertainty about how to interpret them. If more women responded than men (which typically is the case), the result may not change if men and women feel the same way about the question being asked. But if they don't, the overall result may be skewed toward the female point of view.

- **Subjectivity**. A deeper issue of interpretation is the extent to which student testimony is reliable, especially when students discuss how much they have learned. While numerous studies indicate that student self-reports about learning are indeed correlated with direct measures of their learning, those correlations are not very strong. In particular, many students feel confident about their mastery of a subject even before they are really exposed to it, and are unaware of the standards of performance demanded at the college level (concerning such abilities as writing). This is why accrediting agencies insist on *direct* evidence about the attainment of learning outcomes of the kinds discussed in Chapter 2.

Still, self-reports about learning gathered through student surveys can still be valuable to an institution as a cross-check on what direct-assessment approaches are telling us. Furthermore, if students report that they are not learning in a particular area, that may be a red flag. Such a response may signal a problem in learning itself, indicate that the skill in question is not being addressed in the curriculum, or that the students don't understand what is meant by the survey question. Finally, research shows that students are far better at describing their learning *behaviors* than at describing or quantifying *what* they've actually learned. They can usually describe with fair accuracy how much they study, how much contact they have with faculty, and what their learning experiences are like—which makes it all the more important for the institution's analysts to ask about such matters beyond straightforward satisfaction when they seek student opinions.

- **Timeliness**. Alumni surveys carry an additional caveat: The amount of time between when alumni graduated and when they are surveyed is important, especially if the institution has changed in some important ways in the interim. If too many years have elapsed or too many significant changes have taken place on campus, respondents may report on an institution that in some sense no longer exists.

Taken together, these inherent conditions suggest caution in interpreting results. When examining evidence based on surveys, board and committee members should always be provided with the margin of error and level of confidence associated with the results. They should also be aware of the response rate to the survey, as well as what the survey's analysts have to say about how any differences in response rates among different kinds of students might affect interpretation. Board and committee members should look for noticeable differences in responses across different kinds of questions or different kinds of respondents, and should remain aware that particularly in the case of alumni surveys, timeliness is an important factor. Above all, board and committee members should ask administrators and those presenting that data about their views regarding the limitations of the results and whether there is corroborating evidence from a different source.

3. *How are we soliciting and considering external stakeholders' views?*

While students are the most obvious "stakeholders" in academic quality, other individuals and entities consider the quality of academic offerings important, too. Those potential stakeholders include employers, professional associations, community opinion leaders, other institutions that provide transfer or graduate-education destinations, and local citizens. It is important for boards and administrators to understand who their institution's external stakeholders are and how their perceptions might potentially affect the institution.

Still, gathering information from external constituencies is a process that should be treated with caution and forethought since soliciting feedback can be difficult, expensive, and time-consuming. And unfortunately, experience suggests that mailed or Web-based surveys are not the best way to obtain feedback from external constituents. Response rates to such efforts are typically low—partly because it can be difficult for potential respondents to see the connection between the institution and what they do, and partly due to many people's reluctance to fill out a time-consuming survey. So while, for example, area employers may care a good deal about both the technical abilities of local graduates as well as their motivation, responsibility, and teamwork skills, those employers will likely be more comfortable talking directly with institutional representatives about such concerns than filling out a survey.

Thus, quite a lot of initial contact and preparation is generally needed for such efforts to be successful. Ideally, institutions will contact external stakeholder employers well in advance of a survey effort, using letters or phone calls to explain why the institution wants their views and how their input will be used. After that, focus groups and direct face-to-face interviews in the interviewee's own place of business usually are the most effective methods for gathering the desired information. Other approaches include working through established channels such as chambers of commerce or local trade associations.

Academic programs or departments that have established relationships with external stakeholders through program advisory committees may be of particular help in survey work. While such committees are usually formed to advise on curriculum content, their members are increasingly being recruited as "external assessors" to help program faculty determine the adequacy of student work. At the very least, these external representatives should be asked directly about the kinds of knowledge and skills they seek in newly trained employees. In the case of non-vocational disciplines, such as in the arts and sciences, institutions may also wish to recruit external advisory groups composed of disciplinary faculty drawn from other institutions. Even though such disciplines usually do not have formal mechanisms for engaging peers elsewhere, their faculty generally are willing to listen to opinions from their counterparts at other institutions about what should be expected of students at different levels.

> **Student and stakeholder input is an integral part of academic-quality assurance.**

In sum, all board members should be broadly aware of the many ways that their institution might seek student and stakeholder perceptions of academic need and effectiveness. Given the rising public profile of higher education, student and stakeholder input is an integral part of academic-quality assurance, and boards should expect their institutions to be fully and appropriately engaged.

Meanwhile, members of the academic affairs committee should be more deeply engaged in reviewing the evidence generated about student and stakeholder perceptions, and they should work with academic and student affairs leaders to draw out and address any issues that may emerge. Are there patterns of dissatisfaction or systematic discontinuities in student learning experiences? Are they significant enough to constitute a threat to the institution's long-term reputation or ability to attract the kinds of students it wants? Are there patterns of student experience that are especially positive and noteworthy that the institution might exploit more systematically in recruitment and marketing?

The broader perspective that board members can bring to such discussions is frequently more effective in raising issues about what is happening to students and what is important to stakeholders than the narrower and more self-interested perspective of academic leaders. As always, that fact does not mean that board members should forget the distinction between raising and pursuing strategic issues and micromanaging decisions about academic content or the details of student affairs programming. But it does imply that trustees should judiciously examine presented evidence and raise the right questions to ensure that the institution's leadership is paying attention.

Chapter 5

TAKING STOCK
OF PROGRAM ASSETS

In the turbulent world of market competition, corporations have learned that it is wise not to try to be top-notch in everything but to instead develop a set of well-researched strategic priorities that dictate the few areas where true quality lies, and where they should invest the most resources. That does not mean they divest themselves of all other businesses, which may be necessary to maintain for a variety of reasons ranging from strong local markets to the need to protect a brand or reputation. But it does mean that careful planning is required to identify product strengths, weaknesses, and customer demands as well as differential investment in a few high-quality offerings.

Accordingly, every retail business needs to think about its positioning and product line. Some businesses establish themselves as convenience stores, serving a broad local market with a wide but shallow array of everyday wares. Others are department stores, whose customers expect higher quality, greater selection, and an even broader range of available goods. Still others are specialty outlets that depend upon providing a strategically edited range of products to a sufficient mass of customers to keep them in business.

Although higher education institutions clearly differ from corporations or retail outlets, colleges and universities are, in a way, a mix of all three retail types with respect to their principal "stock"—academic programs. What's more, colleges and universities need to engage in a similar kind of strategic thinking regarding positioning. After all, like department stores, most institutions are expected to maintain a given array of academic programs even though some of them are run at a loss. Everyone expects a college or university to have a physics department, just as everyone entering a department store will expect it to sell clothes and dishes. In addition, colleges and universities have general-education requirements that create internal markets for certain programs: All students who hope to graduate have to take an English course or two, for example, whether or not English interests them or is remotely relevant to their academic path.

Unfortunately, both of those pressures keep most institutions from specializing in their best-reputed "product" (that is, academic programs) to the extent many retail businesses can. Still, most colleges and universities have some programs that are better than others, so they would be wise to further market and invest in them to reinforce perceptions of quality. And most also have programs that they should consider scaling back or eliminating entirely.

Determining the optimal size, configuration, and performance of an institution's academic offerings is an essential part of academic-quality management and quality assurance, and thus should also be part of what academic administrators think about when reviewing their array of undergraduate programs. Board members need to ensure that the chief academic officer and senior academic staff are paying attention to such matters, and furthermore need to be aware of the principles, tools, and evidence available for reviewing and assessing program offerings.[15]

■ THE BASICS

Reviewing and Evaluating Academic Programs

Every institution keeps (or should keep) an array of statistics that reveals the overall condition of its academic programs. Most are straightforward—enrolled students by major, numbers of full-time and part-time faculty by rank or category, and classes taught or credits generated—and most are likely to be shared with the board by the institution's chief academic officer.

Examined over time, such data can paint a picture of the changing demands

---

[15] Consistent with Principle 5 of the "AGB Statement on Board Responsibility for the Oversight of Educational Quality" (AGB, 2011): See Appendix, page 112.

for instruction in relation to parallel changes in teaching assets. But actively managing academic programs requires a different way of looking at various statistics. As a result, many institutions construct regular performance ratios to analyze how particular programs are operating. When appropriate opportunities arise, members of the academic affairs committee should ask chief academic officers what kinds of measures they use to monitor program condition and performance on an ongoing basis, and what related issues may be arising.

Many colleges and universities have established systems for academic program review. Most such systems operate on a regular cycle that includes an examination of each program every five to seven years. At public institutions, a periodic program review sometimes occurs simultaneously for a given subject across all units in a system or state so that, for example, all English or all chemistry programs are reviewed in the same year. While patterns vary across institutions, most program reviews also involve the compilation of a detailed statistical summary using various indicators, a written self-study prepared according to a standard protocol by the program's faculty, and an examination of the study and self-summary by an internal peer-review team composed of academic staff and faculty from other disciplines. In some cases, external reviewers from the same field or discipline are included, and their independent reports are made part of the record.

Such program reviews are intended to be comprehensive and to suggest ways in which programs might be improved. Areas addressed by most review protocols, for instance, include an analysis of student demand and future need, enrollment trends, faculty background and preparation, other important resources such as equipment and space, curriculum coverage and structure, and teaching and research activities. Given the increasing attention paid to outcomes by accrediting organizations, such reviews now usually also devote a good deal of attention to results of assessments of student learning. And if the institution has programs that are independently accredited by programmatic accrediting organizations, those external reviews are usually built into the internal program-review schedule to avoid duplication of effort.

Because the primary intent of program review is supposed to be academic improvement, the recommendations for change generated by the process are clearly a key outcome of any review. However, in many traditional academic program reviews, such recommendations grow out of the faculty's self-study, indicating changes that faculty members themselves would like to make and that probably require new resources—a result that has earned the process some criticism because they almost never identify actions that might *save* resources, or programs that might be eliminated. Still, the review process provides a welcome opportunity to check up on the institution's program array on a regular basis, and it can be especially helpful in quality assurance if external reviewers are included.

> "Faculty self-studies almost never identify actions that might *save* resources or programs that might be eliminated."

Occasionally, colleges and universities will perform an in-depth examination of their entire array of academic offerings, all at once, as part of a strategic-planning or budgetary exercise. Such simultaneous review has the virtue of considering common current data and assessing the place and need of each academic program within the curriculum as a whole (in contrast to the more common rolling cycle of program review, in which information about at least some programs is several years out of date). Most institutions undertake such an exercise only when under significant budgetary pressure, and when the primary motive is to find something to cut in order to preserve (or even enhance) programs they consider high-quality or mission-central. It is unfortunate that so few institutions undertake such complete reviews, because this kind of strategic look at the total configuration of academic programs is often useful regardless of the condition of the budget.

■ QUESTIONS FOR BOARDS TO CONSIDER

Examining how and how well academic programs are working is central to the task of academic management. As with any management task, boards should ensure that those responsible are taking it on and using the right tools. The most important questions board members should ask, therefore, are how the institution's academic leadership determines whether the right array of academic programs is in place, and whether new programs should be added or existing programs discontinued. Academic affairs committees, in turn, may delve more deeply by asking whether all academic programs are operating efficiently and achieving intended objectives.

In addition, when issues related to program effectiveness arise in the course of regular board discussion, board and committee members may wish to raise the following questions:

1. *Do we have the right mix of programs?*
It is important for all board members to understand that the natural rhythm of program development at most colleges and universities is not entirely rational. Unlike commercial enterprises, which generally prepare for the launch of a new product with a good deal of research on customer demand, cost of production, and marketability, most academic programs are developed because faculty members want to teach them, and doing so will enhance the professors' own reputations as well as that of the institution. If a new cadre of faculty is hired with a specialization in a particular branch of cell biology, for example, there likely will be new classes offered in this field, and the program may eventually mushroom into a major. (This occurs most often at the graduate level.) This process has been much parodied, but it is not at all atypical.

And it is also not all bad. Academic entrepreneurship is what keeps colleges and universities vital, and branching out into new fields of instruction may well lead the institution in promising new scholarly directions. It may be equally useful, however, for board members—and particularly members of the academic affairs committee—to periodically ask academic leaders how program inventories are monitored and managed. There are several points to listen for when raising such questions.

The first and most important "program mix" question for boards deals with the extent to which the current array of academic programs is appropriate to the institution's mission. Public governing bodies should be especially proactive on this question if an institution appears to be drifting away from its assigned role and scope—by offering doctoral programs at the expense of undergraduate teaching, for example, or by duplicating the offerings of another nearby publicly funded institution.

This question is not asked as often at independent institutions (nor is it safe to assume that it routinely is asked at publics, either). As always, exactly how such topics are discussed in boardrooms is a delicate matter, often because boards stray from strategic questions towards debates about content that are properly faculty territory. This means above all that such discussions should concentrate on the overall *configuration* of the institution's program offerings—its "center of gravity"—and not focus unduly on the details of particular academic programs. For example, to generate revenue, quite a few independent colleges with an original liberal arts mission are now offering professional graduate programs. It is a rational strategy as far as it goes, but boards needs to ensure that the strategy is deliberate and considered, lest their institutions creep toward a mission that was neither planned nor consistent with its true mission and purpose. The board is uniquely positioned to keep such strategic questions at the forefront of presidential attention.

What's more, boards should ensure that academic leaders can identify both the *roles* of specific academic programs in the institution's overall array and the *criteria* that allow the administration to assess whether those programs are filling their purported roles effectively. One scholar of program review, George Keller, observed that the best way for board members to look at an institution's array of academic programs as a whole is to consider them as analogous to a portfolio of investments. In a well-balanced investment portfolio, some securities are relatively low-risk, low-yield, and intended to be held for the long term, while others may be intended to secure short-term gains and yield higher dividends at a somewhat greater risk. A small portion of the portfolio may be in the form of secure assets (such as gold) as an ultimate hedge against downside risk.

When academic programs are viewed as part of an institutional program portfolio, each program should be evaluated on the basis of three key attributes, which academic affairs committees may be particularly interested in discussing with academic and faculty leaders:

- **Mission centrality.** To determine the centrality of any given program, the key questions are: To what extent does the program in question "belong" at the institution, regardless of whether it is large or productive? And is it possible to imagine the institution without it? Examples of genuinely mission-central programs might include computer science at MIT or religious studies at a faith-based college, while programs that might be less mission-central could include majors with very minimal enrollment, or a costly and highly specialized graduate program at a non-elite regional university.

- **Productivity**. Always a key issue at budget time, productivity refers to the efficiency of a program in relation to its cost. Some highly productive programs, regardless of their content, are helpful to their institutions because the "profits" they generate can help subsidize the operations of less-productive programs that are more mission-central. Even so, institutions should try to limit the number of such programs if they lack other desirable characteristics.

- **Quality**. Monitoring academic quality is essential in order to identify both particular areas of strength in the institution's program portfolio and areas where further investment may be beneficial. Still, it is important to understand that while all programs should be above a particular threshold of quality, it is a myth that all programs at a given institution are or must be of "equal" quality with respect to assessed outcomes, faculty background and teaching/research practice, and a host of other factors. Institutional reputations frequently are built on a few academic programs of especially high quality that may be worth subsidizing even though they are not highly productive.

In essence, the art of academic management is to constantly seek improvement in all three areas, while appropriately balancing the overall "portfolio" of program offerings. Academic leaders should be able to explain their reasoning and decision making about academic programming in discussions with the academic affairs committee. And all board members should be aware of those choices whenever a major program investment or termination is under consideration. If what is regarded as a highly mission-central program is about to be closed because it is unproductive or because quality thresholds have fallen, the right decision may be to reallocate resources from more-productive but less mission-central programs to bring productivity and quality back into line. Similarly, if productive programs that are *not* related to mission are scheduled for expansion simply to help the bottom line, boards should raise questions about whether such actions will affect mission-related programs or stakeholders' overall perceptions of academic quality. These are long-term strategic questions that sometimes only boards may perceive as important and that board members have a specific responsibility to pose.

2. *How are we managing program costs?*

Two basic statistics are important in understanding instructional costs at any institution: the *proportion of overall expenditures devoted to instruction* and *instructional costs per student*.

- **Expenditures devoted to instruction**. Roughly speaking, after deducting research and public-service costs (which vary by institutional type), between one-third and two-fifths of every college or university's expenditures goes to support instruction. That proportion may seem surprisingly low to many board members when they first hear it, but it makes sense after one remembers the many expenditures involved in keeping an institution operating (including administrative costs, the operations and maintenance of a large and complex physical plant, and student-support services). But because instruction is the only business that every college and university has in common, boards should carefully monitor the proportion of resources the institution spends on instruction. Indeed, the matter is important enough that some boards have established policies specifying the minimum proportion of the institution's resources to be spent on instructional functions and include this statistic in their annual set of dashboard indicators.

- **Instructional costs per student**. If the percentage of total expenditures an institution dedicates to instruction provides a measure of its *effort* devoted to instruction, costs per student lets administrators monitor the *efficiency* of this effort. Most institutions calculate instructional costs per student on the basis of full-time-equivalent (FTE) students, though the underlying concept is based on costs per credit hour. Instructional costs often will vary across academic programs—and across peer institutions as well—so boards should understand some of the reasons that drive these differences.

  Although some programs will require unusually high investments in equipment or technology, the principal ingredient of instructional costs is faculty salaries in relation to the number of students taught. If a given program is staffed by relatively senior tenured faculty, it naturally will exhibit higher costs than others, just as programs that employ many part-time staff typically will enjoy lower unit costs. Similarly, if the same program suddenly undergoes a significant increase in class size, its instructional costs will decrease. Faculty-deployment decisions thus will affect costs to some extent, but much of the institution's instructional cost structure will be relatively immutable because it reflects the seniority and composition of a fixed array of faculty and a fairly established pattern of historical course enrollments.

Academic affairs committees may look at such cost figures as part of their wider engagement with program review. In examining cost data, committee members should be careful not to jump to conclusions about high-cost and low-cost programs without asking academic administrators to explain differences in fixed assets and structure. Only after those basic questions have been raised and satisfactorily answered is the committee in a position to discuss with academic leaders what the resulting patterns of expenditure and efficiency imply about academic priorities for investment.

Committee members also should know that statistics on costs are usually most meaningful when viewed in comparative terms. As a result, many colleges and universities monitor instructional-expenditure proportions and instructional costs per student against a set of peer institutions that are similar in size, student characteristics, and program mix. At public institutions, moreover, this frequently is done under the auspices of a system office or state coordinating board. Most peer groups of this kind are established to compare faculty salaries and tuition rates—both matters of direct concern that involve decisions typically approved by the board. But they may be useful for other kinds of statistical cost comparisons as well. Consequently, committee members should ask whether such detailed comparisons exist and what institutional leaders think they show.

Further, if such comparisons reveal that the institution's instructional costs are unusually high, committee members should ask administrators why, and whether anything might be done to reduce costs without sacrificing quality. Board members should remember that, despite common perceptions that cost and quality go together, some approaches allow savings in instructional cost without noticeable declines in learning outcomes. Such cost-saving approaches include the following:

- **Targeting a few high-cost programs for restructuring to improve curricular coherence**. If certain programs are not required for degree completion, but have high costs due to high numbers of junior- and senior-level courses, academic administrators may want to determine if the number of offerings is warranted given historic enrollment patterns. The situation may be especially worthy of attention if these courses duplicate content, and may require using peer-group data on instructional costs by department or discipline to identify which programs are targeted and why their costs are out of line in comparison with others. The peer-group data may then suggest ways to reduce those costs—e.g. through larger enrollments, more efficient use of available instructional resources, and substituting lower-cost faculty for higher-cost faculty in low-enrollment classes.

- **Reducing the number of low-demand, upper-division courses offered each term**. As noted earlier, a significant feature of the instructional landscape in higher education is that senior faculty members are often relatively free to decide what and when they teach. Such freedom is a good thing, but should be carefully monitored by academic leaders. Institutions sometimes can realize substantial savings in instructional costs with no difference in ultimate outcomes simply by trimming the undersubscribed courses offered each term that students do not need to complete their programs.

- **Using technology and a redesigned instructional approach in high-enrollment introductory courses**. Every institution has a relatively small number of courses that generate a disproportionate share of the institution's teaching volume. Usually, such courses are introductory ones such as English composition or psychology 101, which are required for all students or by many majors.

  Such courses are good candidates for redesign because any change in marginal cost per student will be magnified substantially. There can be substantial payoffs from using technology to supplement teaching in areas where it is appropriate—such as communicating content or providing students a way to drill or practice their skills—and using peer tutors to displace high-cost faculty in areas where the latter really are not needed.

  The National Center for Academic Transformation, a nonprofit organization that promotes the use of information technology to improve learning outcomes and reduce the cost of higher education, has helped more than 100 institutions redesign their large-enrollment introductory courses in this manner, with cost savings ranging from 20 to 85 percent.

Such strategies can appropriately be discussed with academic leaders during the academic affairs committee's ongoing dialogue about academic costs and quality. Again, however, it is important to stress that running the instructional program is the job of the faculty and academic leaders, not the board. It is both inappropriate and wasteful for boards to try to act alone to identify specific ways to save instructional costs. But board and committee members should be familiar with the basic tools that academic administrators have at their disposal to manage instructional

> **6 6** ...inquire whether staff have researched available good practices to contain costs without sacrificing quality. **9 9**

costs, and their minds should not be clouded by an unquestioned assumption that cost and quality are inextricably linked. Instead, they should be prepared to question such assumptions when they are expressed by faculty and academic administrators, and inquire whether staff have researched available good practices to contain costs without sacrificing quality.

3. *What counts as program quality?*

Chapter 2 discussed what is generally considered the most important aspect of academic quality: the achievement of desired learning outcomes. But faculty members, academic leaders, and external stakeholders may have additional views of program quality, and may consider other sources of evidence to determine its presence. While maintaining a primary focus on learning outcomes, board members—and especially the members of the academic affairs committee—should consistently question those responsible for academic programs about their definition of quality and what they are doing to maintain and improve it. Some of the likely answers include:

- **Reputation.** Although frequently denigrated as a subjective and unimportant factor, a program's reputation among "customers" and peer faculty at other institutions can in fact be important in helping an institution attract the best students, faculty, and external resources such as grants or contracts. "Customers" in this case might include students, faculty of graduate programs at other institutions, and employers. The opinions of peer faculty may be especially important because a program's reputation in the field often determines how easily it can attract and hire the best new professors. That said, reputation is an elusive quality and should not necessarily be taken at face value. Other factors, such as the presence of specific faculty expertise or distinctive curricular features, may lie behind a particular program's reputation; faculty and academic leaders should be able to explain these reasons

- **Admissions selectivity.** A straightforward but important mark of success is a program's ability to attract high-quality students. At selective institutions, factors such as average SAT or ACT scores and high-school rankings and GPAs can be examined across programs. Every faculty wants well-prepared students, so getting them is frequently viewed as a particular earmark of quality.

- **Student satisfaction with their experiences in their majors.** Studies of undergraduate students repeatedly emphasize the importance of the students' experiences in their major fields of study. At most institutions, that experience is determined not only by disciplinary content but also by a range of intangible cultural factors. Some departments are convivial and social, and characterized by unusual levels of student-faculty contact. Others emphasize creating opportunities for "cognitive apprenticeships," such as working with faculty in a research team. Some are especially known for community service or hands-on field work. Student perceptions of the quality of their experiences are frequently important factors in a program's reputation.

- **Distinctive curricular features.** It is not surprising that different kinds of major programs vary substantially in their curricular design across disciplines, but a good deal of curricular variation may also occur across institutions even within the same discipline. Frequently, that is because a program has created curricular features that set it apart. Examples might include a common introductory experience, substantial fieldwork or independent work, a capstone course, or a scholarly thesis. Such features can play a big role in a program's attractiveness and overall reputation among faculty peers.

- **Employer or graduate-school demand.** For programs with a vocational or professional focus, employer demand for graduates is an important metric of quality. Are graduates quickly hired? In what types of enterprises do graduates tend to work? Faculty members in such programs may also wish to solicit feedback about their graduates' less-tangible characteristics—for example, are their graduates "adaptable" and "hands-on"? Such responses may also be obtained from faculty at the students' graduate programs, and may include feedback about the students' levels of preparation, aptitude for graduate study, or specific undergraduate experiences that their graduate professors found attractive.

- **Ability to attract external recognition or resources.** At institutions with a strong research emphasis, a department or program's reputation is heavily influenced by its ability to attract external grant support. A comparable phenomenon exists in undergraduate teaching programs: Have they been recognized as outstanding by their disciplinary associations? Have they participated in funded projects or received grants associated with innovations in teaching or curriculum design? Do faculty members earn recognition through institutional or extra-institutional teaching awards?

How faculty and academic leaders define and recognize program quality is an important factor in their drive to improve it, and academic affairs committee members should listen carefully to what they say. The most important reason is to ensure that discussions about quality improvement are grounded and active, but it is also essential that the faculty's and administration's own definitions of quality are consistent with the institution's overall mission and values. As with more general questions of program mix, there will be a natural tendency among the faculty to want to heighten disciplinary recognition and student selectivity as the most important marks of quality. That should be expected and is for the most part healthy. But committee members need to be sure that all discussions about enhancing quality based only on those two attributes takes place within the appropriate bounds of mission. If there are signs that such disconnects between mission and programming are becoming serious, the committee should alert the full board to follow up with the president.

4. *Who reviews general education?*

As discussed earlier in this chapter ("Reviewing and Evaluating Academic Programs"), program review tends to look at the institution's academic offerings one at a time and in isolation. But some of the most important outcomes of postsecondary education—and many of the aspects that define the distinctiveness of a particular institution—are about more generic attributes of college graduates. As noted in Chapter 2, employers and other external stakeholders especially value such abilities as communication, problem solving, and personal responsibility. Board members—and especially members of the academic affairs committee—may be in a unique position to look at program results more holistically and synergistically, and from a perspective that transcends those of individual academic disciplines.

In this respect, the academic affairs committee may be especially interested in the functioning and effectiveness of the institution's general education program. At most institutions, the general education program will constitute about a third of the undergraduate curriculum, which students will complete primarily within their first two years of study. Committee members should be aware that because discipline-based departments constitute the heart of academic organization, general education programming has fairly weak administrative and leadership support at most colleges and universities. Most department chairs will think first about staffing graduate courses and courses related to the major, and faculty members within the department will, for the most part, thank them for it. And though some institutions have explicitly located responsibility for general education in an office reporting to the chief academic officer, they almost always lack a faculty or resources of their own. As a result, responsibility for assuring the quality of general education is dispersed and frequently ineffective.

Program review of a general education program occurs in several ways. Sometimes a review of a department's "service" courses is included as part of its program review as described earlier. In such cases, academic affairs committee members should ask about what this additional material says about the quality and the relevance of the department's contribution to this important curricular component if this topic is not explicitly addressed. Occasionally, the institution's general education program is made an independent topic of program review, using the same kinds of guidelines applied to other academic programs. In such cases, committee members should ensure that the results of the review have strong administrative backing and will be given the resources needed to implement any recommendations. Most frequently, however, general education simply is not addressed—in which case committee members should explicitly raise the question of who is responsible for assessing and ensuring the quality of general education. If the administration's answers are unclear, the matter needs the attention of the chief academic officer and the president.

In discharging responsibility for ensuring that the quality of the general education program is carefully examined, board members toe a difficult line. Here, as elsewhere, the faculty has responsibility for academic content, and boards ought to stay out of the way. However, it is arguable that general education is where academic programming is closest to institutional mission, especially for liberal arts or faith-based institutions. Every institution's mission statement has something to say about what all of its graduates have in common and how they will contribute to life and society. In the final analysis, it is up to the board to ensure that those statements are meaningful.

5. *How does program review drive program improvement?*

Because the primary purpose of program review is to improve curriculum and pedagogy, boards should be interested in how such improvement occurs. Some board members, through their service on the academic affairs committee, may have participated directly with faculty and academic leaders in discussing review results. But at many institutions, unfortunately, program review has become ritualized to the point that the information it generates rarely is recognized or used. Sometimes that is because program review is a mandated process (particularly at public institutions, where program review is required by state authorities but not actively championed or supported by local academic leaders). Regardless, academic leaders should take advantage of opportunities to look at program effectiveness, or else the resources invested in them are wasted. Boards have a legitimate interest in preventing such waste.

It is worth noting that (1) connections between review processes and program improvements sometimes may be difficult to detect and (2) not all program review results in visible change. Indeed, it has become common for institutional program reviews or assessment processes to be deemed ineffective because it seems that nobody *changed* anything. But in fact, much of the benefit of a review happens inside the program itself in the form of changes in faculty decisions and behaviors that are not reported to anybody else.

A truly reflective faculty will carefully consider what a review has taught them, make any needed changes, and move on. They will request no new resources to implement those improvements, and there will be no written record. And in some cases, the available evidence may show that things are going just fine and that no explicit changes are needed. More subtly, faculty members may tweak the *ways* in which they teach, without necessarily adopting entirely new approaches. After all, many of the benefits of processes such as program review are cultural in this sense and may not be easy to see on the surface. Boards should recognize that a beneficial review process is one in which faculty members are willing to visibly and sincerely invest their own time, which faculty will cease to do if they do not learn anything from the process. It should fall to the academic affairs committee to explore with academic administrators whether any such subtle forms of improvement have occurred.

All board members should also be aware of any formal connections between program review and established institutional decision-making processes. Accordingly, the board should ask questions such as: Are program-review results considered in the institutional-planning process? If so, what kinds of results can be traced? Do those results have budgetary implications? If so, what kind? Indeed, after looking at review results alongside one another, some institutions discover that particular themes repeatedly occur across programs— for example, that multiple programs may be encountering similar challenges in harnessing instructional technology or in implementing experiential learning approaches or pedagogies that emphasize active learning. Such patterns have clear collective implications for faculty development that ought to trigger discussions about greater investments in appropriate workshops or teaching and learning centers.

Despite such benefits, it is nonetheless true that many critics of program reviews see them as little more than channels for departments to ask for new resources. To alleviate such concerns, it is fair for boards to use a review to request evidence to justify any newly requested resources. Doing so can help also set a precedent for well-supported departmental requests, and may help well-justified requests get priority over unsupported ones during budgeting. Once again, though, sensitivity in inquiring about such matters is essential: It is not the board's prerogative to second-guess individual budgetary decisions. But if the overall pattern of responses by academic leaders suggest that assessment and review processes are not connected to decision making (a condition, experience suggests, into which colleges and universities unconsciously may sometimes drift), the board needs to remind academic leaders of their responsibility.

> " Too often, key quality processes are pursued as independent activities. "

The board should further ensure that all four of the foregoing processes—assessment, retention management, soliciting student and stakeholder opinion, and program review—are working together as part of a larger institutional approach to planning and decision making. Too often, these key quality processes are pursued as independent activities by different actors with different motivations and intentions. Apart from the president, board members are among the few individuals who can determine whether those processes are connected to one another to systematically inform investments and strategic decisions. If there are doubts about whether this is occurring often enough, board members have an obligation to raise the issue with the president and insist that the matter be addressed. Integration is something that boards clearly understand and act upon in the realm of fiscal affairs, in which revenue generation, resource allocation, and fiscal accountability must be properly combined to ensure responsible budgeting and financial management. It ought to be equally understood and acted upon by boards when they discharge their responsibility for academic affairs.

ACCREDITATION:
THE QUALITY TEST

The topic of institutional and program accreditation brings the discussion of the board's role in academic quality assurance back to the notion of fiduciary responsibility. Accreditation, the established "quality test" for the academy, performs much the same role in an institution's academic operations as a financial audit does in its fiscal affairs. That parallel is worth delineating along several dimensions.

First, like a successful audit, a favorable accreditation decision provides a clear public signal to stakeholders and potential customers that the institution and its academic programs operate with integrity and have attained a recognized level of performance that can be relied upon. Like a financial audit, a clean bill of health is the expected and usual outcome. But negative findings, though they occur infrequently, can spell real trouble: Loss of accreditation means loss of funding through participation in federal student financial-aid programs and sends a strong market message to potential students that the institution either is untrustworthy or its programs are of inferior quality. Boards must ensure that administrations never allow a loss of accreditation.

Second, the accreditation process is focused principally on an institution's methods for ensuring quality and integrity. A financial audit effectively certifies through external review that the institution conducts its fiscal business according to generally accepted accounting procedures and that, therefore, its fiscal statements and claims about its bottom line can be trusted. Accreditation, in essence, performs the same function regarding claims about academic quality—especially with respect to the achievement of acceptable student-learning outcomes. Accreditors will rarely make explicit statements about the overall quality of student learning exhibited by the institution's graduates. Rather, by examining *how* colleges and universities verify their own claims about learning, accreditors assess the level of confidence and trust that external observers should place on these claims.

Third, there are two sets of results following an accreditation process:

- **A public declaration of the institution's accredited status.** Similar to the contents of a financial audit report, the public notice of accreditation is a straightforward determination of the institution's standing.

- **A confidential team report and action letter.** These documents, which accompany the public declaration of accredited status, contain some of the most valuable information available from the accreditation process. Like a "management letter" that accompanies a financial audit, a confidential report and action letter advise the institution privately about matters of concern to which it ought to attend promptly to avoid future difficulties with accredited status. Accreditation action letters can address a range of topics, but some of the most important will focus on improvements that should be made in academic quality-assurance processes. Boards should pay particular attention to them to be sure they understand what accreditors are saying and that academic leaders are addressing these issues. [16]

Fourth and most crucially, an accreditation visit is an opportunity for the institution to learn. Far too many presidents and program directors view the accreditation process in much the same way they view financial audits: that is, as a burden that must periodically be endured to maintain a "Good Housekeeping Seal," but that represents a diversion of resources away from core functions. Adopting such a compliance-only mentality is a mistake for two reasons. First, such apathy is often noticed by accreditors, who are looking for genuine engagement in the

---

[16] Consistent with Principle 7 of the "AGB Statement on Board Responsibility for the Oversight of Educational Quality" (AGB, 2011): See Appendix, page 107.

review process as an important marker of a "quality culture." More important, a half-hearted approach to accreditation means that an institution will approach the process as though it is wasting resources on something that adds no value. But such an approach is both futile and potentially harmful to the institution. If accreditation is a required activity that entails institutional costs, and if the process can be harnessed by the faculty and academic leaders to reveal solid information about how academic programs are functioning and how they can be improved, then clearly the institution should take full advantage. Fortunately, accrediting organizations frequently structure their reviews to allow institutions to do so. Boards should know this and should be prepared to ask institutional leaders about these possibilities and how the institution can take advantage of them.

■ THE BASICS

Institutional vs. Programmatic Accreditation

Accreditation comes in two flavors: institutional and programmatic. While both are important, they differ in focus and consequences.

- *Institutional accreditation* is a uniquely American approach to quality assurance that began as a voluntary review process about a century ago, when individual colleges and universities needed a mechanism to accept one another's degrees and credits. Institutional accreditation is currently governed through seven separate, independent commissions located in six geographic regions of the country that also happen to be membership organizations made up of the institutions they accredit.

- *Programmatic accreditation*, or specialized accreditation, looks at individual academic offerings in occupational or professional fields, usually under the auspices of an accrediting commission established by a professional association that governs the conduct of the profession as a whole. Institutional accreditation is centered in and owned by the academy, while programmatic accreditation usually is not.

The review process undertaken by both institutional and programmatic accrediting organizations typically involves three steps:

1. **A comprehensive self-study** prepared by the institution or program according to guidelines provided by the accreditor;

2. **A multiday visit by an accreditation team** of peer reviewers comprising faculty and administrators who prepare a report to the accrediting commission that examines the institution or program against standards established by the commission; and

3. **A commission action** that either continues the institution or program's accreditation and/or imposes sanctions and offers recommendations.

For many years the established institutional accreditation cycle was 10 years, but most regional accreditors have begun adopting shorter cycles. Programmatic accreditation cycles, meanwhile, tend to be about three to five years. There has been a general trend among all accreditors to ask about progress in meeting recommendations and/or to undertake limited site visits "off-cycle" to look at particular issues. Except for the accreditation decision itself, the process typically is confidential, and most accrediting organizations consciously construct their engagement with institutions as consultative, not as an agent of accountability.

Institutional accreditation's interest in quality has always been comprehensive, embracing matters including the adequacy of resources, the appropriateness of institutional-governance arrangements, faculty qualifications, and quality of instruction. That interest has been pursued for more than a century and continues to be important for visiting teams today. But with the Higher Education Act (HEA) of 1965, institutional accreditation was assigned a new high-stakes role by the federal government as the gatekeeper for institutional eligibility to participate in such federal financial-aid programs as Pell Grants and guaranteed student loans.

Through the HEA, Congress has tasked institutional accreditors with determining the answers to two questions on behalf of the federal government:

1. Does each institution have the fiscal and organizational infrastructure in

place to ensure that it can serve as a trustworthy steward of federal funds?

2. Are the institution's academic offerings of sufficient quality that students will benefit from them (and be in a position to pay off their loans)?

Since they assumed this "gatekeeping" role, institutional accreditors increasingly have been asked to review matters related to the second question—including, most prominently in recent years, the quality of student-learning outcomes.

Programmatic accreditation, by contrast, always has been more narrowly focused. Certainly programmatic accreditors are interested in the basic institutional infrastructure within which programs operate. But they are far more interested in whether the program they are looking at is adequately supported by the institution with respect to resources and whether the program is given a fairly free hand in how it operates and governs itself—two concerns that sometimes make presidents ambivalent about programmatic accreditation. On the one hand, achieving accredited status in a professional program such as business or engineering may enhance the program's marketability and therefore its ability to generate revenue. On the other hand, the program's leaders often will use the need to maintain accreditation as leverage for requesting increasingly more resources and operating independence at the expense of the institution as a whole. Boards, as "keepers of the mission," need to understand these dynamics, as institutions can sometimes become overly concerned with satisfying the narrowly conceived interests of programs that can mobilize such leverage. Boards should also understand that while institutional accreditation is something the institution cannot do without, the decision to seek or maintain programmatic accreditation is essentially a management issue centered on marketing and program-investment priorities.

Changes In Accreditation Practice

In the last decade, many institutional accreditors began separating their compliance-enforcement role from their role in providing institutional consultation and improvement. The primary force behind that change was pressure from colleges and universities whose basic accreditation status was not at risk; those institutions had grown weary of what appeared to be costly and ritualistic reviews that added little to their campus-planning and management processes.

The result is a far more flexible review approach that gives institutions ample opportunity to use the accreditation process to engage a set of quality issues of their own choosing. This will happen only if presidents are aware of these opportunities and decide to act on them. Boards, too, should be aware of such opportunities, and see to it that, if present, they are appropriately recognized and acted upon.

Institutional accreditation is also becoming more oriented toward accountability—a change most apparent in accreditors' requirements about reporting retention/graduation rates and evidence of student-learning outcomes. In the past, accreditors looked primarily at the adequacy of institutions' processes for gathering evidence about learning; now, they are at least as interested in examining actual levels of performance and whether they are good enough. This makes it all the more important for institutions to seek external benchmarks and peer comparisons for such measures.

> **66 Accreditation is becoming more transparent... most accreditors are developing short public reports outlining institutional strengths and weaknesses. 99**

Finally, institutional accreditation is becoming more transparent with respect to public reporting. In the past, only the accreditation decision was made public. Now, most accreditors are developing short public reports outlining institutional strengths and weaknesses.

The Board's Role in Accreditation

Boards should be aware that institutional accreditation standards frequently require their own participation in the accreditation process, and that the effectiveness of the institution's governance arrangements—including the scope and delivery of board oversight—will be part of what is examined. As a result, board members should be familiar with the standards addressing governance established by their institutional accreditor and the specific roles boards are expected to play (and not play) in institutional and academic governance.

Well in advance of an accreditor's visit, board members should review past accreditation results and know that trustees are expected to be broadly aware of the administration's plans to address any recommendations that result from a review. Most accreditation visits also feature meetings with the board chair and/or selected board members to discuss how the board functions in its oversight role. Board members should expect such meetings to include questions about the board's awareness of the institution's key academic quality-assurance processes—and should be prepared to answer such questions if they arise.

Myths About Accreditation

Finally, board members should be aware of the many persistent myths about what accreditors "really want" with respect to learning assessment. One such myth is that only standardized tests are credible to accreditors as evidence of student learning. Institutions and programs frequently assume that standardized exams will satisfy review teams because of their perceived rigor and public credibility. While such tests may indeed be appropriate to particular kinds of learning and in particular programmatic contexts, accreditors are actually seeking instances where faculty members have chosen assessment approaches that match the types of learning being emphasized and that generate results that are both usable and used. So long as an institution's or program's approaches generate useful and credible information, accreditors will not favor any particular method.

Similar myths surround the use of qualitative-assessment approaches or those based on expert and peer judgments of student performance. Despite prevalent rhetoric, "measurable" outcomes are not always what accreditors are looking for. But perceptions are correct that external reviewers are seeking direct evidence of student academic achievement, so assessment programs based solely on student-satisfaction surveys will likely receive negative comments from a visiting team.

■ QUESTIONS FOR BOARDS TO CONSIDER

At the most basic level, boards should be broadly aware of the institution's accreditation status, the institution's current place in the accreditation cycle, and the most important issues that arose during its last accreditation visit. Board attention to programmatic accreditation is appropriately less salient, but the board should at least know which programs at the institution are accredited by such organizations, and be aware of plans to seek accreditation for other programs if doing so is an emerging goal.

Beyond such basics, the following questions related to accreditation may be useful for boards to pursue:

1. *What progress have we made in addressing recommendations from the last review?*

One frequently voiced reservation about institutional accreditation is that it operates on a very long cycle. Although most institutional accreditors contact colleges and universities more frequently than once every 10 years, such mid-cycle contact usually involves only a limited review or a focused visit to follow up on a specific concern. As a result, there is some tendency for faculty and staff to heave a collective sigh of relief after reaffirmation occurs and not think much about what needs to be done until it is time to gear up for the next review.

The recommendations that usually emerge from an institutional review tend to be systemic, raising such issues as administrative infrastructure and communication, governance, diversity, and strategic planning—issues that often take some time to address. As a result, it is prudent for boards periodically to ask the institution's leadership for an update on outstanding concerns that arose from the last accreditation review, what is being done to address those concerns, and what progress has been made. This need not be a lengthy activity, but should occur annually on a regular schedule.

From a larger perspective, institutional leaders need to acknowledge that when they complete an accreditation cycle, they probably know more about their

institutions than ever. Typically, institutional self-studies have compiled, organized, and examined enormous bodies of data about finance, enrollment trends,
instructional resources, and program assets that are otherwise seldom examined
in such a comprehensive fashion. Similarly, most institutions use the occasion of
accreditation to conduct a range of additional studies such as student and stakeholder surveys, alumni or employer studies, or special assessments of student
learning. Because of the size and scope of institution-
al self-study, such a level of evidence gathering and
analysis is impossible to maintain indefinitely. But it
ought not disappear entirely.

> 66 Ask institutional leaders
> how they plan to sustain
> the momentum for
> planning and evaluation
> generated by the impetus
> of accreditation. 99

Unfortunately, many institutions allow the planning and evaluation assets built through their self-
studies to atrophy once an accreditation cycle ends. That means that the extensive (and expensive) apparatus must be reconstructed from scratch when the
next accreditation cycle comes around. Not only is that wasteful, it also prevents
continuity in the evidence that may be examined over time—for example, posing
some of the same questions to alumni in the same way so that trends can be established. (Fortunately, in an effort to prevent such information loss and inefficiency,
newer alternative accreditation approaches emphasize doing fewer things with
respect to evidence and analysis, but doing them more consistently over time.)

Boards should be aware of this common cycle of intensive self-study followed
by atrophy. They should also, at the conclusion of an accreditation encounter, be
prepared to ask institutional leaders how they plan to sustain the momentum
for planning and evaluation generated by the impetus of accreditation. Boards
have several options at their disposal to help them work with campus leaders. For
example, presidents should be asked to review the results of an institutional accreditation review with the board soon after its conclusion and to discuss explicit
plans for addressing its recommendations. One part of the review might include
determining which bodies of evidence to maintain over time for strategic-planning purposes and to help prepare for the next accreditation visit. Briefly reviewing progress on these plans each year with the board might be made a regular ex-

pectation. Similar provisions addressing accreditation might be included in the board's annual review of presidential performance and be established as expectations for new presidents.

This last point may be especially important in the light of decreasing average presidential tenures: A new sitting president may not have presided during the last accreditation visit and may be unfamiliar with the issues previously raised and discussed. Boards should therefore ensure that brief progress reports addressing the last accreditation review's recommendations are built into the board's annual calendar. New presidents should also be reminded early in their tenure (or even during the search process) of past commitments to maintain strategic-planning assets made by their predecessors. They also should be asked how they intend to discharge or modify these plans.

2. *What progress have we made in assessing student-learning outcomes?*

Regardless of whether the topic of assessing student-learning outcomes was explicitly cited by an accreditation review team—and it usually is these days—boards should pay special attention to ensuring that faculty and academic leaders continue to address it. Accrediting organizations will continue to move decisively toward ensuring that institutions' processes for assessing student learning are central in reviews of academic-quality assurance.

As discussed in Chapter 2, accreditors increasingly expect every academic program to have visible statements of learning outcomes, to collect credible direct evidence that those outcomes are being achieved, and to demonstrate how the resulting information is being used to improve teaching and learning. Accreditors will have the same expectation for general education and other cross-cutting curricular requirements. Knowing that assessment practice is still relatively new in higher education, accreditors have given institutions time to put such mechanisms into place, and up to now they have been relatively lenient in enforcing their assessment standards. But because the federal government is increasingly holding accreditors themselves accountable, that leniency situation cannot and will not continue. Boards should be fully advised that continuing inattention to assessment involves risk to their institutions.

3. *Are our accreditable programs accredited? Should they be?*

Programmatic accreditation can be a mixed blessing for colleges and universities. On the one hand, the external recognition provided by accreditation can enhance a program's reputation and marketability. These are substantial advantages, and if the programs are accreditable by a recognized professional body, they will always benefit from achieving accredited status. But is seeking all possible instances of programmatic accreditation good for the institution? The fact is, programmatic accreditation can carry a substantial price tag with respect to direct costs and the organizational "overhead" associated with responding to a large and diverse array of external review bodies. At a large university, for example, it is not unusual for programmatic accreditors to pay three or four visits each year.

More subtly, maintaining accreditation may require the institution to invest scarce resources in things that may not be consistent with established mission or planning priorities. For example, accreditation standards in some fields may mandate a particular student-faculty ratio, require faculty to engage in a specified amount of recognized research, or call for investments in special facilities that are inconsistent with what the institution is doing for equally important but non-accreditable academic programs. These are important trade-offs, and board members should be aware of them.

Members of the academic affairs committee may play a more explicit role in advising on the strategic choices involved in seeking or maintaining specialized accreditation. Members should know which of the institution's programs are in fact accredited by a professional body as well as those that could be but are not. In some cases—in most programs in health-related fields, for example—programmatic accreditation essentially is required: Individuals must be graduates of an accredited program in order to practice. But in other prominent professional fields, such as business or engineering, accredited status is not required. In still others—teacher education, for example—requirements for accredited status vary by state. And in fields such as business and nursing, there may be several programmatic accreditors to choose from when seeking recognition.

Under such conditions, the decision to seek or maintain programmatic accreditation is complex and needs to be understood on a case-by-case basis. But it is important for academic affairs committee members to recognize that, with the exception of those few programs where accreditation is a requirement, program accreditation is a *business* decision that should be made after carefully weighing the associated costs and benefits. Academic affairs committees may provide presidents and academic leaders with useful advice on how to approach this decision from a disinterested standpoint—"above the fray" of academic politics. Above all, when they provide such advice, board members should do so from the point of view of their prime role as "keepers of the institution's mission."

4. *What do we hope to learn from our engagement with accreditation?*

Institutional and programmatic accreditation represents a considerable and, to some people, surprising investment of institutional resources. A medium-size college or university routinely devotes the equivalent of two full-time administrative staff positions to the process, and must also allow involved faculty members substantial release time during the two years or so they are preparing for institutional reaffirmation. The direct costs of the process can easily total six figures. It is, of course, a necessary price to pay for remaining in good standing with the federal government and the academic community, and it probably represents a good marketing investment as well—but again, institutions are not getting their money's worth from the process of self-examination afforded by accreditation if they treat it simply as a routine compliance exercise. One of the most important questions board members should ask when the time for institutional reaccreditation rolls around, therefore, is how the administration plans to use accreditation as an opportunity to learn and improve.

Virtually all of the regional commissions that accredit institutions allow institutions flexibility to address topics of their own choosing. In some cases, that flexibility is built into the process—for example, in the Quality Enhancement Plan required by the Commission on Colleges of the Southern Association of Colleges and Schools, or in the processes selected for continuous review and improvement under the Higher Learning Commission's AQIP approach, which is based on the Malcolm Baldrige National Quality Award. Boards of institutions operating under either auspice should know the particular topics the institution has selected for in-depth study and the reasons why these topics were chosen.

Institutions taking more flexible approaches such as these must demonstrate that they meet all established accreditation standards by submitting documents and exhibits that show compliance. Increasingly, in fact, such basic compliance reviews occur off-site, with no campus visit required. Instead of writing a traditional descriptive self-study narrative that systematically addresses each accreditation standard, institutions prepare an analytical document that examines in depth two or three topics previously approved by the accreditation commission. Examples might include the effectiveness of an undergraduate first-year experience program, improving retention and success among students of color, or creating a more student-centered learning environment.

Accreditors, however, expect most of the topics to be related to the core task of undergraduate education in the realm of teaching and learning. Academic affairs committees may be especially helpful in providing academic leaders with advice about which topics to choose because they are focused primarily on the strategic questions the institution needs to answer about its academic programs. They also may be in a good position to assess which potential topics are the most symbolically powerful in demonstrating the institution's strengths and distinctiveness to outside stakeholders.

Board members also should know that there are sometimes good reasons why the institution's leadership may not want to pursue a novel approach to institutional review. Such alternative approaches are, after all, most applicable and useful for colleges and universities that already are in a fairly strong position with respect to accreditation and already have all the needed documentation to quickly fulfill the compliance portion of a review in order to get on with its topical component. Other, less-well-positioned institutions may benefit more instead from adopting a traditional accreditation approach. A traditional approach will still allow those institutions the opportunity to exercise the effort and discipline required to document that internal quality-assurance processes such as assessment, course and program approval and review, and faculty promotion and tenure are in place and effective.

Furthermore, precisely because the new approaches to institutional review are more flexible and open-ended, they also are more uncertain. Presidents know that when they engage in such reviews they will need to work carefully with the accrediting organization to delineate the scope of the visiting team's inquiry: With fewer guidelines to constrain them, visiting team members sometimes can become "loose cannons," so adopting the safer traditional approach to self-study may be an appropriate choice. For those and other reasons, a president may elect not to take advantage of some of the newer and more flexible approaches to review that accreditors now offer. The boards should know the reasons for the president's decision, and a wise president will seek the board's counsel about it. And, even if a more traditional course of action is adopted, the board should continue to pose the question of how the institution plans to take advantage of the accreditation opportunity as a learning experience, however it is structured.

> **" All boards should remember that academic accreditation is a uniquely American practice that needs their support. "**

Finally, all boards should remember that academic accreditation is a uniquely American practice that needs their support. In most other countries, responsibility for ensuring and maintaining the quality of colleges and universities rests with a government ministry, which typically pays for higher education as well. In the United States, that responsibility is vested collectively in the higher education enterprise itself. The legal and operational independence that results has allowed our higher education system to become the most diverse and entrepreneurial in the world—and, most would still say, the best.

American higher education will be able to maintain this status only if the academy takes seriously its historic role to maintain its own integrity through the self-regulatory process of institutional accreditation. Boards have a clear responsibility to their institutions to ensure that they are operating with integrity and delivering high-quality academic programs. But they have an equally important collective responsibility to the nation to make certain that self-regulation remains a reliable guarantor of academic quality and integrity. This means being aware of the process at their own institutions, and it occasionally may mean asking hard questions. Allowing accreditation to become empty and ritualistic is a sure invitation for excessive government regulation, which could be unhealthy for academic vitality. In their collective role of custodians of the academy, boards should be perpetually wary of this possibility and do their best to keep self-regulation vital.

EPILOGUE

For 14 years, I was privileged to serve as a board member at Truman State University in Missouri, an institution that has a long tradition of assessing student learning and making use of the results to improve instruction. Truman State has had a succession of fine presidents who have kept these matters at the forefront of the institution's agenda, and I am proud that the university has been cited on several occasions for its exemplary efforts by its regional accrediting organization. But in my "day job" as a consultant and commentator on higher education accountability and instructional improvement, I am forced to admit that far too few presidents or institutions have made these matters of high priority.

As Derek Bok, distinguished former president of Harvard University, once wrote in an essay on the board's role in academic affairs:

> Presidents are the natural source of initiative to see that problems of student learning are identified and reforms are developed. In practice, however, few presidents have made serious, sustained efforts to play that role. Perhaps they fear opposition from their faculties or adverse publicity if they discuss weaknesses in their institutions' educational programs. Perhaps they are too busy balancing budgets and raising money. Certainly the easier course is to direct their energies toward more visible and less controversial goals, such as increasing average SAT scores or building imposing new facilities.
>
> Do trustees have a role in overcoming this weakness? Surely not by taking it upon themselves to evaluate the quality of education and to recommend improvements. Such actions would exceed their competence and antagonize the faculty. A better course would be for trustees to ask the president to report on current procedures for assessing the effectiveness of the faculty's teaching and for developing better ways to educate students. ...
>
> Once the trustees have received answers to their questions, they

can urge the president to work with the faculty to make the college a more effective learning organization and to report periodically on the results. By so doing, trustees would not presume to dictate how professors should teach their courses. But trustees would give the quality of education a much higher place among the college's priorities. Presidents would receive a powerful mandate to press ahead with programs of assessment and experimentation rather than succumb to the forces of inertia and indifference that so often stifle such initiatives....

If priorities are to change to put greater emphasis on the quality of education, someone will have to alter the incentives and rewards that currently influence academic leaders. No one but the trustees seems capable of accomplishing that result.[17]

These are wise, though provocative, words. Achieving the proper balance in advocating for academic-quality assurance and improvement will be a perpetual challenge for every board—but such advocacy is indeed a part of every board's basic responsibility. It is my fond hope that this book will provide committed board members with a place to start and a few resources to continue this important task.

As a final note, I am deeply gratified by the many positive responses that I have received regarding the first edition of *Making the Grade*. Since it came out in 2006, I have used it to ground many board retreats on the topic of academic quality and continue to receive comments on the helpfulness of the advice provided from both board members and presidents. I sincerely hope that this second edition of what has become known as "The Little Yellow Book" will be equally well received.

—*Peter T. Ewell*

[17] Bok, Derek, "The Critical Role of Trustees in Enhancing Student Learning," *Chronicle of Higher Education*, December 16, 2005.

AGB STATEMENT ON
BOARD RESPONSIBILITY FOR THE OVERSIGHT OF EDUCATIONAL QUALITY

INTRODUCTION

A governing board is the steward of the institution it serves. As a fundamental part of its stewardship, the board is responsible for assuring the larger community and stakeholders to whom it is accountable that the education offered by the institution is of the highest possible quality. Yet AGB's 2010 survey on the engagement of boards in educational quality revealed that board members often are not sure how to provide stewardship in this area, and some even doubt that they should.

In AGB's book *Making the Grade: How Boards Can Ensure Academic Quality*, Peter T. Ewell affirms that the oversight of educational quality "is as much a part of our role as board members as ensuring that the institution has sufficient resources and is spending them wisely." The educational mission of colleges, universities, and systems makes this a primary obligation for their boards, and the significant fiscal investments made by these institutions, by their students and donors, and by state and federal governments underscore its importance. Governing boards should recognize that assuring educational quality is at the heart of demonstrating institutional success and that they are accountable for that assurance.

The current environment makes this responsibility more pressing. Today's technological, pedagogical, and economic forces, along with increasing public skepticism about the value and cost of education, make board accountability for quality crucial. And with only 38 percent of America's adult population now holding a degree from a college or university, it is clear that much more needs to be done if we are to ensure the country's economic and civic future.

Our efforts to confront that contemporary reality for higher education are complicated by a number of formidable challenges, including:

- A significantly older and more ethnically and racially diverse student body;
- Increasing numbers of contingent faculty members;
- Revenues that have not kept pace with institutional need;
- Dramatic escalation in demand for admission while certain fixed costs are skyrocketing, straining institutional capacity;
- Competition for students, faculty members, and resources that diverts available funding away from educational quality and toward less critical functions;
- Tension between issues of workforce preparation and intellectual development;
- Large numbers of students needing remedial courses; and
- Declining confidence that higher education is capable of meeting its commitment to students and its obligation to serve the public good.

Some of these challenges directly affect educational quality; others intensify the need for institutions to demonstrate quality. If we are to effectively broaden opportunity and increase success among our students, then we will need to address these challenges head-on and with some urgency.

Board Accountability

AGB's "Statement on Board Accountability" asserts, "[A governing] board broadly defines the educational mission of the institution, determines generally the types of academic programs the institution shall offer to students, and is ultimately accountable for the quality of the learning experience." While academic administrators and faculty members are responsible for setting learning goals, developing and offering academic courses and programs, and assessing the quality of those courses and programs, boards cannot delegate away their governance responsibilities for educational quality. The board's responsibility in this area is to recognize and support faculty's leadership in continuously improving academic programs and outcomes, while also holding them—through institutional administrators—accountable for educational quality.

In fulfilling this responsibility, the board should work within the governance structure of the institution. For some boards, significant change may be required in how they interact with academic administrators and faculty members on matters of educational quality. AGB's "Statement on Institutional Governance" stresses that "Governance documents should state who has the authority for specific decisions—that is, to which persons or bodies authority has been delegated and whether that which has been delegated is subject to board review." Governing boards should make a conscious effort to minimize ambiguous or overlapping areas in which more than one governance participant has authority, particularly in the area of educational quality, where faculty members, administrators, and the board all have important responsibilities.

This "Statement on Board Responsibility for the Oversight of Educational Quality," approved by the Board of Directors of the Association of Governing Boards (AGB) in March 2011, urges institutional administrators and governing boards to engage fully in this area of board responsibility. The following seven principles offer suggestions to promote and guide that engagement.

PRINCIPLES

1. The governing board should commit to developing its capacity for ensuring educational quality.

According to AGB's survey on boards and educational quality, a little more than one-third of board members receive information related to oversight of educational quality during their board-orientation program. Additionally, while most have experience on boards of either corporate or nonprofit organizations, they are less familiar with academic trusteeship. To fulfill this specific area of oversight responsibility, a board should commit to a strategy for educating itself.

Board leadership and senior administrators should intentionally incorporate discussions of educational quality in new-trustee orientation programs, board education programs, and the annual agendas of the board and its various committees. Structured discussions with faculty members, key administrators, and outside experts on learning goals, as well as reviews of the institution's current student-learning assessment practices, student retention and graduation rates, and information about program and institutional accreditation, can help develop the board's understanding of these issues.

Both the board and its appropriate committees (for instance, the Academic Affairs or Education Committee and the Committee on Student Affairs) must make understanding the elements of educational quality a central feature of their agendas. Adding regular reports on student-learning outcomes to those that the board already receives on finances and endowments will round out the board's understanding of its essential oversight responsibilities.

2. The board should ensure that policies and practices are in place and effectively implemented to promote educational quality.

The board is ultimately responsible for the currency of policies and their implementation, including policies related to teaching and learning. With the president and chief academic officer, the board, either through an appropriate committee or as a body, should ensure that institutional practices for defining and assessing educational quality are current, well communicated, and used for continuous improvement of students' educational experience. The board should receive reports—annually, if not more often—on the appropriateness of these practices, their results, and any changes needed.

Because faculty members are responsible for the important work of setting standards for educational quality, creating and implementing processes for assessment, and responding to the findings, the board should encourage a focus on these responsibilities in new faculty orientation and through faculty development programs. Additionally, the board should ensure that faculty work on learning assessment is recognized and rewarded.

3. **The board should charge the president and chief academic officer with ensuring that student learning is assessed, data about outcomes are gathered, results are shared with the board and all involved constituents, and deficiencies and improvements are tracked.**

Practices in assessing student learning differ from institution to institution based on mission and experience. A board needs to understand how assessment is done at its institution, what the educational goals are, whether the goals align with the institutional mission, and how well the institution performs against those goals. And the board should understand the challenges associated with measuring learning, especially those dimensions of education that are less easily quantified.

With leadership from chief academic officers, board committees—where they exist—should delve more deeply into student-learning assessment practices and findings. Involving faculty leaders in these discussions is critical in conveying the board's support for the endeavor and its commitment to quality.

A board committee, such as the Academic Affairs or Education Committee, should provide the board with policy-level, strategic summaries of the assessment information it receives. It should report regularly to the full board on the learning-assessment data collected, the significance of the data, institutional responses to those findings, and improvements over time.

4. **The board is responsible for approving and monitoring the financial resources committed to support a high-quality educational experience.**

Ordinarily, the delivery of educational programs is the largest institutional expense. Also, because an institution's finances are directly tied to enrollment, retention, endowment, and external support of its programs, boards should monitor regularly the connections between academic programs and financial sustainability. The board should advocate for sufficient resources in support of educational priorities. It also should monitor the cost effectiveness of financial commitments to these priorities and be certain that the investments are consistent with institutional mission, plans, and overall financial trends. Boards of public institutions, which may lack the authority to determine overall institutional funding levels, should help make the case for sufficient state support of educational quality.

Although improved educational quality is not necessarily the result of increased spending, the board should consider the allocation of new funding or the reallocation of existing funding to address academic needs identified through learning assessment, program review, or reaccreditation. Additionally, the board should encourage and be prepared to invest in academic innovation, including the development of new delivery models, to advance the institution's educational mission. Institution-wide efforts to contain expenses can help to facilitate investment in academic program priorities. On occasions when a board is required to make decisions about academic programs based on financial circumstances, it is best done with candor and consultation with stakeholders.

To be fully accountable, the board needs information about the institution's educational outcomes to assure the public, students, parents, donors, and other funders of the return on their investment of tuition dollars, philanthropy, and state and federal aid. The board should ensure transparency in reporting this information to stakeholders.

5. The board should develop an understanding of the institution's academic programs—undergraduate, graduate, and professional programs.

An institution fulfills its mission primarily through its academic offerings—its general education program, academic majors, and degree programs. To ensure that the mission is being met, board members need to understand the broad structure of these offerings. Orientation for new board members should include an overview of undergraduate, graduate, and professional degree programs. Boards should be aware of how the mix of programs reflects the institution's history, is suited to its mission and student profile, and compares to those of peers and competitors. The board should also be aware of the learning goals the institution has established for students.

Also, because an institution's finances are directly tied to enrollment, endowment, and external support of its programs, boards should monitor regularly the connections between academic programs and financial sustainability.

6. **The board should ensure that the institution's programs and resources are focused on the total educational experience, not just traditional classroom activity.**

With few exceptions, a student's education involves more than classroom experience and the formal curriculum. It also includes a range of learning experiences and academic-support activities outside class that have proved to have significant effect on student development, education, retention, and graduation. An understanding of an institution's educational quality includes an appreciation for the value added by such experiences beyond the classroom.

The board should develop a holistic understanding of the opportunities and services that the institution provides to complete students' educational experience. Some of these—for instance, internships, learning communities, student-faculty research opportunities, and service learning—can be among the most distinguishing features of an institution. Boards should be informed about the quality of these experiences and other support activities, and their effect on students' learning as well as on recruitment and retention.

7. **The board should develop a working knowledge of accreditation— what it is, what process it employs, and what role the board plays in that process.**

Accreditation—the periodic, peer-based system of review of higher-education institutions and programs—is designed to assure the public of an institution's commitment to academic quality and fiscal integrity. It also serves to stimulate continuous improvement by the institution.

As part of its attention to educational quality, the board should become familiar with how accreditation works at the institution. The board's own ongoing educational program should include an overview of the accreditation process, the various types of accreditation that the institution holds, and the key findings from accreditation processes. The board should also be clear about its role in the institutional accreditation process. Most regional accreditors require contact with members of the board, and some include standards for the effectiveness of board governance.

The board should require from senior administrators a timely preview of forthcoming re-accreditation processes and periodic progress reports on the required self-studies. It should review key elements of the accreditation self-study, the visiting team's report, and formal action and decision letters from the accrediting organization, and it should consider their implications for the institution's strategic goals, mission, and resources.

RECOMMENDATIONS TO STAKEHOLDERS

For Institutional and System Chief Executives

- Work with board leadership to ensure that educational quality and student-learning assessment are part of the agendas of the board and its appropriate committees, and that sufficient time is provided for discussion.
- Be sure that orientation programs for new board members include a conversation about educational goals and student-learning trends and challenges.
- Encourage the chief academic officer to foster full board engagement in discussions of matters related to educational quality; assist him or her in understanding board governance responsibilities.
- Working with the chief academic officer, establish goals related to educational quality and learning outcomes to serve as benchmarks for the institution and for the chief executive officer's performance.
- Include the board in the accreditation process in appropriate ways; be certain that the board remains informed as to current accreditations held by the institution as well as the status of anticipated accreditation reviews.
- Remain transparent with the board as to risks and opportunities facing the institution related to educational quality and outcomes, including the link between fiscal and educational decisions.

- Provide regular opportunities for discussion with the board on how the campus defines educational quality.

For Board Members

- Become informed about the board's responsibility for overseeing educational quality.
- Expect to receive strategic-level information and evidence on student-learning outcomes at least annually, including longitudinal data from the institution and, where appropriate, periodic comparisons with peer institutions.
- Hold institutional administrators appropriately responsible for goals that were mutually established for educational quality.
- Use information from the accreditation processes, program reviews, and the assessment of student learning to inform decision making, including financial decisions.
- As appropriate in board and committee meetings, ask strategic questions related to educational quality—goals, processes, outcomes, improvements, trends, and any adjustments needed to improve results.
- Recognize that faculty members and academic administrators shape the approaches to assess the outcomes of student learning, and that boards should not micromanage this work, but that the board is ultimately responsible for ensuring that assessment takes place and that results lead to action for improvement.
- Make service on your board's Academic Affairs Committee part of a regular committee rotation for board members.
- Include the chair of the Academic Affairs Committee as a member of the board's Executive Committee.
- Where possible, consider including one or more academic experts, such as former presidents, administrators, or faculty members from other institutions as ex officio members of the committee charged with oversight of educational quality.

- Schedule opportunities for the Academic Affairs Committee and the full board to discuss educational quality and learning outcomes.

For Chief Academic Officers

- Contribute to the orientation and continuing education of board members regarding academic programs, student-learning goals, assessment practices, and educational quality.
- Working with the board or relevant committee, create a board-level set of dashboard indicators related to educational quality. Update it regularly and present it to the board for discussion annually.
- Work collaboratively with the chair of the Academic Affairs Committee to set a committee agenda that emphasizes institution-specific academic questions and concerns, as well as a review of important academic policies and procedures.
- Ensure that academically related information for the board is clear, concise, free of jargon, and at a strategic level.
- As appropriate, include representatives from the faculty and academic administration in board and committee discussions of the institution's educational goals, approaches for measuring student learning, and progress against goals over time.

Questions For Boards to Ask

- How does this institution define educational quality? In addition to measures of student learning, what is considered in answering questions about educational quality?
- Does the institution say what and how much students should learn? Where is this said?
- What kinds of evidence does the institution collect about learning?
- Is the institution benchmarking performance against external standards as well as tracking institutional performance over time?
- How are assessment results used?

- What do students and alumni say about the quality of their educational experience?

- How do the institution's retention and graduation rates look over time, and how do they compare to those of other institutions?

- What does success look like for the types of students enrolled at this institution?

- Does the institution define college readiness, that is, the skills and knowledge that students must possess to be successful at the institution?

- How do faculty members and administrators keep abreast of innovative ideas for curriculum redesign and teaching?

- What progress has been made in addressing recommendations from the last accreditation review?

- What can the institution learn from its engagement with accreditation?

- Do financial allocations reinforce academic priorities as necessary and appropriate?

- In meeting its oversight responsibility for educational quality, is the board functioning at the policy level or trying to micromanage specific educational programs?

THE ACADEMIC AFFAIRS COMMITTEE OF THE BOARD: AN ILLUSTRATIVE CHARGE

Boards with standing committees should have a committee charged with oversight of educational quality. Such committees have traditionally been called the Academic Affairs Committee, but they go by other names as well, such as the Education Committee, the Educational Excellence Committee, and a range of others. They may or may not be combined with student life or student development committees.

Each board committee needs a charge that clearly identifies the scope of its responsibilities. For the purpose of simplicity, this illustrative charge is for an Academic Affairs Committee.

Illustrative Charge

The Academic Affairs Committee facilitates the governing board's ultimate responsibility for educational quality. It does this by working closely with academic leadership and by regularly monitoring the following:

- learning goals and outcomes;
- program quality, institutional and program accreditation, and program review;
- student retention, graduation rates, graduate school acceptances, and job placements;
- policies and procedures related to faculty compensation, appointment, tenure, and promotion— and when appropriate, the committee makes recommendations for action;
- academic planning;
- the structure of the academic programs—and when appropriate, the committee reviews proposals for adding, modifying and deleting programs; and
- budgets for academic programs and services.

The committee should report regularly to the board and frame recommendations on matters of policy, quality, and funding that require the board's consideration and action.

The committee must receive appropriate and timely information and data to meet its responsibilities. Working at the nexus between board oversight and academic prerogative, the committee should recognize and respect the central role of the academic administration and faculty in academic planning, curriculum development, faculty development, the evaluation and academic advising of students, and recommendations for faculty appointment, tenure and promotion. However, the committee must also be mindful that, in its oversight role, the board is ultimately accountable for ensuring educational quality.

REFERENCES AND RESOURCES

Adelman, Clifford. *Answers in the Toolbox: Academic Intensity, Attendance Patterns, and Bachelor's Degree Attainment.* Washington, DC: Office of Vocational and Continuing Education, U.S. Department of Education, 1999.

Adelman, Clifford. *The Toolbox Revisited: Paths to Degree Completion from High School Through College.* Washington, DC: Office of Vocational and Continuing Education, U.S. Department of Education, 2006.

Adelman, Clifford; Peter Ewell; Paul Gaston; and Carol Geary Schneider. "The Degree Qualifications Profile." Indianapolis, IN: Lumina Foundation, 2011.

American Association of State Colleges and Universities. "The Graduation Rate Outcomes Project." Washington, DC: American Association of State Colleges and Universities, 2005.

Association of Governing Boards of Universities and Colleges. "AGB Statement on Board Responsibility for the Oversight of Educational Quality." Washington, DC: Association of Governing Boards of Universities and Colleges, 2011. (*See Appendix.*)

Association of Governing Boards of Universities and Colleges. "Faculty, Governing Boards, and Institutional Governance." Washington, DC: Association of Governing Boards of Universities and Colleges, 2009.

Association of Governing Boards of Universities and Colleges. "How Boards Oversee Educational Quality." Washington, DC: Association of Governing Boards of Universities and Colleges, 2010.

Basken, Paul, "Quest for College Accountability Produces Demand for Yet More Student Data," *Chronicle of Higher Education,* May 17, 2012.

Bok, Derek, "The Critical Role of Trustees in Enhancing Student Learning," *Chronicle of Higher Education,* December 16, 2005.

Ewell, Peter T.; Karen Paulson; and Jillian Kinzie. "Down and In: Assessment Practices at the Program Level." Urbana, IL: University of Illinois and Indiana University, National Institute for Learning Outcomes Assessment (2011).

Kazin, Cathrael and David G. Payne, "Ensuring Educational Quality Means Assessing Learning," *Trusteeship,* March-April 2009.

Kuh, George and Stanley Ikenberry. "More Than You Think, Less Than We Need: Learning Outcomes Assessment in American Higher Education." Urbana, IL: University of Illinois and Indiana University, National Institute for Learning Outcomes Assessment (NILOA), 2009.

Kuh, George D.; Jillian Kinzie; John H. Schuh; Elizabeth J. Whitt; and Associates. *Student Success in College.* San Francisco: Jossey-Bass, 2005.

Loughry, Andrea, "So Many Rankings, So Few Measures of Student Learning," *Trusteeship,* January-February 2008.

McDonough, Patricia M.; Anthony Lising Antonio; Mary Beth Walpole; and Leonor Perez. *College Rankings: Who Uses Them and with What Impact?* Los Angeles: Graduate School of Education and Information Studies, University of California at Los Angeles , 1997.

Morrill, Richard L. *Strategic Leadership in Academic Affairs: Clarifying the Board's Responsibilities.* Washington, DC: Association of Governing Boards of Universities and Colleges, 2002.

Organisation for Economic Cooperation and Development, "Education at a Glance 2011," Paris: Organisation for Economic Co-operation and Development, 2011.

ABOUT THE AUTHOR

Peter T. Ewell is vice president of the National Center for Higher Education Management Systems (NCHEMS), a research and development center in Boulder, Colo. founded to improve the management effectiveness of colleges and universities. Ewell was a member of the Board of Governors of Truman State University in Missouri from 1996 through 2010.

Ewell's work focuses on assessing institutional effectiveness and the outcomes of a college education. He is involved both in research and direct consulting with institutions and state systems on collecting and using assessment information for planning, evaluation, and budgeting. A staff member since 1981, he has directed many projects on assessment, including initiatives funded by the W.K. Kellogg Foundation, the National Institute for Education, the Consortium for the Advancement of Private Higher Education, and the Pew Charitable Trusts. He chaired the design team for the National Survey of Student Engagement (NSSE) and serves as the chair of the National Advisory Board for both NSSE and the Community College Survey of Student Engagement.

In addition, Ewell has consulted with more than 375 colleges and universities and 24 state systems of higher education on such topics as assessment, program review, enrollment management, and student retention. He also has been actively involved in NCHEMS work on longitudinal student databases and other academic-management and information tools.

Ewell has written seven books and numerous articles about improving undergraduate instruction through the assessment of student outcomes. Among his books are *The Self-Regarding Institution: Information for Excellence* (National Center for Higher Education Management Systems, 1984) and *Assessing Educational Outcomes* (Jossey-Bass, 1985), both of which have been widely cited in the development of campus-based assessment programs. More recently, he is the author of *U.S. Accreditation and the Future of Quality Assurance* (Council for Higher Education Accreditation, 2008) and was one of four authors of the *Lumina Degree Qualifications Profile* (DQP).

Before joining NCHEMS, Ewell was coordinator for long-range planning at Governors State University. A graduate of Haverford College, he received his Ph.D. in political science from Yale University in 1976 and was on the faculty of the University of Chicago.

ASSOCIATION OF
GOVERNING BOARDS
OF UNIVERSITIES AND COLLEGES

About AGB's Mission:

In today's environment, knowledgeable, committed, and engaged boards are central to the success of colleges and universities. AGB helps board members and college and university leaders address governance and leadership challenges by providing vital information, fostering effective collaboration, building board capacity, and serving as a trusted advisor. Our programs, publications, meetings, and services offer a range of ways to improve board governance and institution leadership.

Who are AGB Members?

AGB counts the boards of over 1,250 colleges, universities, and institutionally related foundations among its members. Boards join AGB to provide resources for exceptional governance to board members and senior staff. The 36,000 individual board members and institutional leaders AGB serves come from universities and colleges of all types (independent and public, four-year and two-year, general and specialized) as well as foundations affiliated with public universities.

How Can You Engage?

AGB membership extends to every individual member of the board and selected members of the institution's administration. By virtue of their institution's membership in AGB, individuals receive access to all of AGB's services, knowledge, and real-time solutions to pressing governance and leadership issues.

AGB members become more engaged in their roles; they gain access to vital information, benefit from the expertise of our skilled staff and consultants, and are better able to support their institution's application of key principles and practices of higher education governance. Explore the benefits of AGB membership and further support your institution's mission. Start by visiting *www.agb.org*.

AGB has many members-only resources online. For log-in information and password access, visit *www.agb.org* or contact: dpd@agb.org